PRAISE FOR *Troy Steven's*

BREAKING BIPOLAR

"Breaking Bipolar by Troy Steven is a no-holds-barred view of bipolar disorder. Steven offers riveting first-hand descriptions of his own episodes and those of people he interviewed. Steven provides an aggressive action plan to manage One's symptoms and life in general, covering everything from creating a balanced medical protocol to selecting compatible psychiatrists. This refreshing book is a boon to persons with bipolar disorder, professionals in the field, and interested friends and family members."

—*Ellen Bowers, PhD*

"This book is a must read for anyone struggling with bipolar illness. It is also an excellent resource for healthcare providers to use as a structural template to help patients organize their care. Concise, well organized and interesting enough to keep you reading."

—*Scott Meithke, MD*

"I will tell you what is most appreciable, at least in my opinion, about the book, Breaking Bipolar. It in no uncertain terms addresses the subject of the true nature of bipolar medication. This is perhaps the most pressing subject regarding the treatment and management of bipolar disorder. Patients, their family members, friends and even the doctors are rarely found to be completely satisfied with prescribed medication. This results in a lot of pain to everyone. This is an excellent resource for patients and caregivers."

—*S.K. Ditka*

"Breaking Bipolar is exactly what a person who lives with bipolar disorder needs! As a therapist, I see how this disorder wreaks havoc on a person's entire life. Bipolar Disorder is an "emotional cancer"—once someone knows they are in an episode it is often too late to stop the damage. That's why having a well thought out plan can help tremendously in identifying and preventing an oncoming episode. It will be the first book I recommend to my bipolar clients."

—*Ken Kuhn*

"Having served as a mental health counselor/therapist for over 30 years, I find this self-help book to be dynamite. It contains all the elements I would ever suggest that such a book should contain. The author describes an episode in such detail you can sense you are there—authentic and transparent. He gets to the core of why these episodes are serious—LIFE AND DEATH SERIOUS."

—*Dr. Gary J. Butler*

D1559193

Breaking Bipolar

BREAK THE HOLD BIPOLAR DISORDER
HAS OVER YOUR LIFE

Troy Steven

Battle Press
SATELLITE BEACH, FLORIDA

Breaking Bipolar
Break The Hold Bipolar Disorder Has Over Your Life

Battle Press books may be ordered through booksellers or by contacting:

Battle Press
1588 Highway A1A #B
Satellite Beach, FL 32937
1-919-218-4039
www.breakingbipolar.life

Because of the dynamic nature of the internet, any web addresses or links contained in this book may have changed since publication and may no longer be valid.

ISBN: 978-1-5136-5044-9 (softcover)
ISBN: 978-1-5136-6037-0 (hardcover)
ISBN: 978-1-5136-5026-5 (eBook)

Library of Congress Control Number: 2020904114.

Cover Art By M. Aku RoDriguez.

Second Edition

Contents

Dedication

This book is dedicated to the men and women throughout the ages who, despite being bipolar, carved their way
to greatness.

I would like to also dedicate this book to my children
Jennifer, Rachel, Jeremy, and Natalie, as well as my
grandchildren Braelynn and Karmella, who are a constant source of inspiration.

Thanks

First and foremost, I must thank John, Ruth, Gary, Scott, and Jane who graciously agreed to be interviewed about their experiences and struggles with bipolar disorder. Their advice, stories, and wisdom are included throughout the pages of this book, illuminating the reality of being bipolar.

I would also like to express my gratitude to the many people who have seen me through the writing of this book by providing support, exploring ideas, offering constructive comments, and assisting in the editing and proofreading process.

Introduction

I wrote this book with the intent of helping those who are suffering from bipolar disorder, as well as to help myself. Bipolar disorder is a condition that cannot be ignored or underestimated. The implications are simply too serious: suicide or living a crippled, limited life, reckless or violent behavior, financial problems, personal and professional relationships undermined, loss of self-respect, and sometimes most tragically, giving up on your dreams.

The first step is accepting that you aren't alone. Consider this list of many notable individuals who have survived and thrived with symptoms of bipolar disorder. Note that they are listed in alphabetical order because bipolar disorder doesn't discriminate based on gender, race, income or upbringing: Ludwig Van Beethoven; Russell Brand; Drew Carey; Jim Carrey; Dick Cavett; Winston Churchill; Kurt Cobain; Salvador Dali; Jean-Claude Van Damme; John Denver; Charles Dickens; DMX; Richard Dreyfuss; Patty Duke; Carrie Fisher; Larry Flynt; Harrison Ford; Vincent Van Gogh; Halsey; Ernest Hemingway; Kay Jamison; Billy Joel; Meriwether Lewis; Abraham Lincoln; Kristy McNichol; Marilyn Monroe; Isaac Newton; Florence Nightingale; Jane Pauley; Edgar Allan Poe; Theodore Roosevelt; Brooke Shields; Ben Stiller; Sting; Ted Turner; Mark Twain; Mike Wallace; Robin Williams; Owen Wilson; Virginia Woolf; and Catherine Zeta-Jones (Bhandari, 2020), (Bhatia, 2018), (Bailey, 2019).

Remember that these are only some of the people who are brave enough to admit that they are bipolar or are known to have coped with symptoms of bipolar disorder. Millions suffer daily. Struggling alone, oftentimes afraid to confess to others or confront their condition, too many go unnoticed and untreated until it's too late.

Unfortunately, I must include myself in this list. I am bipolar, having struggled since 1993 and I am all too aware of what it takes to confront and battle this illness. I have survived three major episodes, which have resulted in three separate visits to psychiatric hospitals, one due to a suicide attempt. All the while, I maintained a career in engineering, obtained a master's degree, and currently work as an aerospace engineer. I am also the proud parent of four awesome kids, and blessed with two grand-children. This goes far beyond me, though.

The idea of creating a bipolar battle plan began after I attempted suicide in 2007. I almost succeeded. Afterward, I promised myself I would do anything and everything I could to keep it from happening again. I realized I had to make major changes in the way I was managing the illness, in my treatment plan, and in the way I was living my life.

With hopes to help others, I have had to confront my darkest thoughts and demons in order to write this book, which has not been easy. I actually attempted to take my own life. Today I have found balance and achieved security by creating a battle plan to overcome bipolar illness. I have successfully used the plan over time to remain episode free and advance toward achieving my dreams.

Everyone is different, but this disorder and how it affects us is predominantly consistent. We experience ups and downs some-times so severe that feeling utterly average would be welcome. Good days, waking without that uninvited guest lurking, waiting to pounce—sometimes seem so rare. It is a struggle to gain the trust and respect of others, but most of all, to trust that things will get better, that this episode will pass, yet there will be an-other battle in the future. There are no quick fixes. Accept that this is a lifelong struggle requiring immediate attention and long-term remedies.

The book you are holding in your hands promises one thing: to provide you the weapons and training to fight bipolar illness strategically, intelligently, and as a warrior. Equipped with a battle plan to combat bipolar disorder you will be well-armed to achieve victory. This is your life – you don't get another!

Resources:

1. The final pages of the book can be used as a journal to jot down personal notes on ideas and emotions that may pop into your head while reading. Fill these pages with any questions or concerns that arise, and they will become invaluable to revisit over time as well as provide a tangible way of tracking how your battle plan has evolved and changed you and your life.

2. Always remember there are help lines with people on call at all times. Some examples include the National Suicide Prevention Lifeline (1-800-273-8255), the Mental Health Hot Line (1-844-549-4266), and the Substance Abuse and Mental Health Helpline (1-800-662-4357). There is also the Crisis Text Line (Text 'HOME' to 741741). Most importantly, if you are in trouble and your life is on the line, dial 911.

3. Most of you have a cell phone, tablet, or computer. There are a number of available Apps for battling bipolar disorder that you may find to be helpful. For example, "The Best Bipolar Disorder Apps for 2019" can be found at the website:

    https://www.healthline.com/health/bipolar-disorder/top-iphone-android-apps#imoodjournal

"I wish I knew why I am so anguished."
—Marilyn Monroe, Actress, 1926–1962
Believed to have had Bipolar Disorder

Chapter 1

What's At Stake?

Startling Bipolar Statistics

"Dyin' ain't much of a livin', boy."

Clint Eastwood, The Outlaw Josey Wales

Your life could be at stake, and you are your own worse threat. Studies show that up to 20% of people with bipolar disorder end their life by suicide, and 20-60% of them attempt suicide at least once in their lifetime (Dome, 2019). It is unbelievably tragic that one out of five of us end our own lives!

Besides suicide, other catastrophic outcomes of bipolar episodes can include:

- Physical violence (Foundations Recovery Network, 2020).

- Self-mutilation (WebMD, 2020).

- Financial disaster (Sauer, 2016).

- Loss of job and damage to career (Bowden, 2005).

- Loss of spouse or romantic partner (The Bledsoe Firm, 2017).

- Alienation of children (Legg, 2019).

- Loss of friendships (Kildare, 2020).

- Loss of self-respect (Propst, 2019).

Bipolar disorder can be extremely detrimental to your physical health as well:

- Bipolar disorder results in 9.2 years reduction in expected life span (National Institute of Mental Health, 2019).

- Approximately 25% of bipolar individuals are obese (McElroy, 2002).

- More than 40% percent of people with bipolar disorder struggle with alcohol and drug abuse (Cerullo, 2007).

- Bipolar individuals are three times more likely to be diabetic than the general population (Thompson, 2010).

- Bipolar disorder and physical health are closely linked, with risk factors such as weight gain, metabolic syndrome, smoking, and diabetes contributing to cardiovascular disease and early death (Young, 2013).

In her book *Madness: A Bipolar Life*, Marya Hornbacher captures the essence of bipolar disorder:

"Here's the hell of it: madness doesn't announce itself. There isn't time to prepare for its coming. It shows up without calling and sits in your kitchen. You ask how long it plans to stay; it shrugs its shoulders, gets up, and starts digging through the fridge. In the early years, it's like a switch flips on, and though only a moment before you were totally sane, suddenly you have gone mad. But as you learn to manage madness, you begin to notice sooner that it's on its way (Hornbacher 2009, 225)."

The following is my own story about a bipolar episode I had in 2007. I remember becoming manic over a several day period. I started sleeping infrequently, developed racing thoughts, quit eating and believed everything that happened was an omen. My mania began to escalate and I stopped going to work and quit taking all of my medications. A few days later I made a suicide attempt by swallowing all of the pills I had of Lithium and Seroquel. After taking the pills I laid down on the couch and passed out. About an hour later, I regained consciousness because I heard piano music coming from the apartment above me and came to my senses enough to call 911. It terrifies me to this day that I wouldn't be alive today had I remained unconscious.

The Hospital Roof: Episode from Hell

Our army of 24,000 men and 800 chariots marched all night and just before the break of dawn stopped a mile away from the enemy camp. Our advance scouts had estimated the size of the enemy force to be 50,000 soldiers. Battle troops of 6000 men and 200 chariots each were stealthily deployed encircling the enemy fortifications. Suddenly trumpets sounded from the enemy camp. Recognizing we had lost the element of surprise, King David shouted out the command to attack. I knew we were badly outnumbered, but I put it out of my mind, made the sign of the cross, and sallied forth to battle running full speed toward the advancing enemy along with my fellow foot soldiers. The ground began to shake and then our forces met. I killed four enemy soldiers with my spear before two of them tackled me to the ground. Each of them sliced off one of my wrists with their sword and then left me lying there to die. I felt the most excruciating pain imaginable as my arms became slick with blood—unending, unrelenting, the worst hell I ever imagined.

I woke up in a hospital bed feeling like my arms had been cut off. They were purplish, and I remember thinking I had new arms attached, and I noticed an IV attached to the left one. It was then that I remembered what happened. Thank God, I thought, I still had my real arms, it was a nightmare, it didn't really happen. I then carefully checked out the rest of me: wiggled my toes, flexed my knees, and lifted my head off the pillow. I felt for my penis with my right hand, and I felt something coming out of its tip. My heart accelerated to top speed and adrenaline began to flow like lava from an erupting volcano. Lifting the covers I saw a plastic tube entering the urethra. My enraged eyes followed the tube to see where it went, finding a bag filled with yellow fluid I recognized as urine.

"What is going on?" I yelled.

A pretty black nurse came through the door of my room. She noticed that I was looking under the covers and said, "It's a catheter tube. How are you feeling?" She checked the IV that was connected to my left arm, writing on her clipboard as she examined me and chatted away, adding, "You sure did give us a scare." She told me the doctor would be in soon to talk to me.

My mind scrambled to remember how I had gotten to the hospital. It was such a blur… then it hit me like a sledgehammer. I had swallowed all of the pills in my bottles of

Lithium and Seroquel. The next thing I could remember was being wheeled on a stretcher into the emergency room of the hospital. I lay on the stretcher for a little while, and then a nurse walked toward me with a needle in her hand. When I saw her face, I recognized her. The irony—she had slept overnight on my couch a few nights earlier. I had met her and her girlfriend at a bar and asked them to come back to the pool at my apartment complex and swim. I had great sex with her hot friend in my bedroom while this "nurse" with the needle slept on my couch. I had no clue at the time, re-membering her saying that she worked in a women's prison. But there she was, masquerading as a nurse getting ready to plunge a needle into me. I freaked out, jumped off the cart, ran around the corner, and crouched down with my back against the wall. A security guard yelled, "Hey!" and started running toward me. The image of him running around the desk and coming toward me was the last con-scious memory I have prior to waking up in the hospital room. I must have resisted. One guy could not have subdued me, not in that state. I thought to myself I must have been restrained with hand-cuffs, that's why my arms were a dark purple and blue color.

The nurse came back into the room and removed the cathe-ter tube—quick pain, then relief and a sense of freedom. Once more, the nurse said the doctor would be in to speak to me soon. Then she smiled at me and left. Everything seemed out of sorts. I tried to get it straight in my head but was still confused. I had attempted suicide, been trans-ported to the hospital in an ambulance, freaked out when I recognized the nurse in the ER as the prison guard who had slept on my couch a few nights earlier, had my wrists hacked off fighting in a Holy War, and woke up in a hospi-tal room with a catheter tube in my Johnson and an IV in my arm. Where was the freaking doctor?

I looked at the open window. It was about six feet high and didn't have a screen. I decided to vamoose. So I yanked the IV needle out of my arm. All I was wearing was hospital pants, with no shirt or shoes. I got up out of bed and went to the window. I used the crank handle to open it as much as possible and then grabbed the window with both hands and pulled as hard as I could. There was a loud creaking of metal on metal, something broke loose, and the window opened wide enough for me to slip through. At that moment, a couple of nurses came running through the door of my room yelling, "What are you doing?"

I slipped out of the window and stepped down about two feet onto the flat roof of the hospital. It was rock-and-roll time, and I ran like the wind. After about twenty or thirty strides, however, I was out of roof. Looking down and seeing a seven foot drop to the roof below, I decided there was no stopping me now. I jumped, landed barefoot, dropped and rolled, and kept running. I then ran out of roof again, and it was about a twelve-foot drop to the ground this time. I got down by turning my body backward and easing myself down so that I was holding onto the edge of the roof with my hands and then dropped to the ground below. Onward I went, tearing ass across the parking lot toward the adjacent neighborhood.

I was free!

I was picked up later that day by the police and taken to a psychiatric hospital where I was involuntarily committed. As a result of this catastrophic episode, I realized that I needed a plan to stop another disastrous bipolar episode from happening, and most importantly, to stay alive. The result became my ideas for this book, Breaking Bipolar, through creating and utilizing an effective battle plan and sharing it with others.

"Winners never quit and quitters never win."
—Ted Turner, Media Mogul
Diagnosed with Bipolar Disorder

Chapter 2

The Good Stuff

The Good Stuff

O kay, enough bad news! Let's get to the good stuff. Embracing your life while also recognizing your challenges can be one of the most empowering feats of all.

Take heart in the fact that when bipolar episodes are not occurring, individuals with bipolar disorder are busy living their lives, often excelling at their professions, being moms, dads, or students, just like anyone else. In fact, many bipolar individuals currently living or who have lived in the past will be remembered as successful individuals who left legacies of greatness and fame.

Despite a deep depression throughout his life, Abraham Lincoln saved the United States and freed millions from chains; Winston Churchill summoned the strength to inspire a world at war, never bowing to the Nazis or depression; Beethoven gave us the most moving music ever to grace ears; Van Gogh and Dali blessed our eyes with surreal paintings, so bright and expressive; Ernest Hemingway captured a lost generation in words; Edgar

Allan Poe channeled his demons to give us tales of horror; Florence Nightingale pioneered battlefield nursing; while Marilyn Monroe reinvented the notion of beauty. The people who make us laugh out loud are oftentimes bipolar, including Ben Stiller, Drew Carey, and Robin Williams. Look around—bipolar people are striving daily; despite their condition, they are bringing the best out of themselves and reaching their full potential. They have carved their paths through life, and so can you.

A study published in the *Journal of Affective Disorders* in February 2011 found that having bipolar disorder may enhance specific psychological characteristics that are generally viewed as both valuable and socially beneficial. The authors reviewed eighty-one studies that noted positive characteristics and identified five qualities associated with bipolar patients, including creativity, realism, spirituality, empathy, and resilience. The conclusion was that encouraging an appreciation of the positive aspects of bipolar disorder could help combat the stigma and improve patient outcomes (Ghaemi, 2011).

Positive Personality Traits Common to Bipolar Individuals

Creativity: The link between bipolar disorder and creativity is well established. Visual arts, performing, writing, and music—bipolar talent in all of the arts is common and sometimes exceptional.

Exuberance: Exuberance is an abounding, ebullient, effervescent emotion. It's a celebration of the passion and joy in mania and hypomania. It's contagious, starting with that person who makes everyone smile.

Emotional Perspective: What goes up must come down—and then go back up again. Viewing life and issues from both ends makes bipolar individuals more philosophical about the meaning of things. It also gives them a point of reference they didn't have before and that people who lack the perspective of the ups and downs will never understand.

Depth of Experience: You will not meet more experienced, well-traveled, multidimensional people. They have exceptional and often unusual stories to share. People with bipolar disorder, who are so often adventurous, tend to be high achievers and leaders with above average intelligence.

Hyper-sexuality: Lust is also a prominent feature of mania. People with bipolar disorder tend to be dazzling, passionate, and adventurous lovers.

Depression: Surely you are wondering—what can be positive about depression? Light needs shadow, and the most profound understanding includes both. People with bipolar disorder are complex and can illuminate the whole human experience.

Resilience: After suffering through tragic bipolar episodes, bipolar individuals' act of resurrecting themselves gives them the resilience to handle most anything else that may come their way throughout life.

Courage: Tied in with bravado and grandiosity, at its most severe, courage can entail dangerous risk-taking. Yet at its best, courage is rare, inspiring, and heroic.

Recognizing Our Rare Abilities

We have created masterpieces, won wars, and led countries. Is this condition really holding us back? Some have succumbed to the challenge—Robin Williams comes to mind immediately, while the vast majority of us have achieved a "new normal" to lead the lives we have always wanted. What is unique to bipolar individuals is the reality that our condition, once controlled, can give us enhanced abilities, strength, and an unrelenting attitude to achieve far more.

A broken bone heals much stronger than before; a soldier's mettle is tested in battle, making them come out more capable. Once aware of our condition and its challenges, we can then become aware of the early signs and confront this illness. No longer naïve, we are ready for all of life's challenges and its myriad opportunities.

"Without victory, there is no survival."
—Winston Churchill, 41st British Prime Minister
Believed to have had Bipolar Disorder

Chapter **3**

Create Your Bipolar Battle Plan

Ｈow do we battle a mental illness that has the ability to take control of our thoughts and emotions and cause our minds to deceive and betray us? How do we overcome an illness that has the power to cause us to attempt suicide, become violent, and spend money recklessly, not to mention act in so many other destructive ways? How do we surmount the health issues attributed to bipolar disorder such as a shorter life span, obesity, diabetes, and abuse of drugs and alcohol?

The best solution is to follow a lifelong battle plan that is based upon the expert recommendations of the medical community. The consensus is that successful treatment of bipolar disorder depends on diligently following a comprehensive treatment plan including medication, educating yourself about the illness, communicating with your psychiatrist and therapist, having a strong support system, and helping yourself by making healthy lifestyle choices (WebMD, 2020).

This chapter guides you through the process of creating your personal bipolar battle plan. It explains the planning process, how to establish your goals and objectives, enemy reconnaissance, selecting your weapons, warrior training, and becoming a bipolar warrior.

I don't claim to be an expert. I make decisions based on whether I am experiencing bipolar symptoms, the state of my mental and physical health, financial well-being, status of my relationships with my significant other, children, family, and friends, and level of satisfaction with my job and my career. If changes are needed, I make adjustments to my battle plan. Each of you will have different circumstances and challenges than I do, so you should tailor your battle plan accordingly.

Bear in mind that you are the General of your own individual bipolar battle plan. You must become an expert at treating your own disease. Live by the motto, *Bipolar Heal Thyself.*

The Planning Process

Planning ahead is how we deal with most challenges in life. Understanding the planning process will aid you in creating your battle plan. The planning process is shown in the figure below:

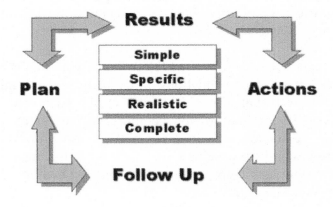

THE PLANNING PROCESS

As you go through the process of creating your bipolar battle plan, ask yourself the following questions:

1. Is the plan simple? Is it easy to understand and to act on? Does it communicate its contents easily and practically?

2. Is the plan specific? Are its objectives concrete and measurable? Does it include specific actions and activities?

3. Is the plan realistic? Are the goals realistic? Nothing stifles implementation like unrealistic goals.

4. Is the plan complete? Does it include all the necessary elements?

Even if it passes all of these criteria, you will need to refine and make improvements to your battle plan on an on-going basis, depending on what is working for you and what is not working. The success of your plan depends on your level of commitment and involvement, as well as your ability to adapt to changing circumstances.

You are engaged in an undertaking of major importance to you. To be sure of success you must have plans that are faultless. If the first plan which you adopt does not work successfully, replace it with a new plan, if this new plan fails to work, replace it with still another. And so on. Be persistent. Your achievement can be no greater than your plans are sound.

Establish Your Goals and Objectives

The first rule of combat is to believe in your reasons to fight, which are your goals and objectives. This is the key: you have to believe that you WILL win. Not that it will happen, but that it should happen and that you are in charge.

When establishing your goals and objectives, consider your deepest wants and desires, your dreams, and what you want to achieve before leaving this great earth. Don't limit yourself—you deserve the best of everything!

Consider the following questions when setting your goals and objectives:

1. What motivates me?

2. What interests me?

3. What would I do more of if I could?

4. What do I care about?

5. Where do I want my life to go?

6. What brings me joy?

7. What are my dreams and desires?

The goals and objectives I set for my bipolar battle plan include:

1. Never again attempt suicide.

2. Effectively deal with any bipolar symptoms or side effects that may occur.

3. Eliminate bipolar episodes.

4. Maintain strong mental and physical health.

5. Establish lasting financial security.

6. Be in a romantic relationship with an intelligent, desirable woman who enjoys my company as much as I enjoy hers.

7. Continue to enjoy and foster good relationships with my kids, extended family, and friends.

8. Laugh out loud on a regular basis.

Know Your Enemy

"Know your enemy and know yourself and in a 100 battles you will never be in peril."

—Sun Tzu, The Art Of War

Bipolar disorder is a very complex disease. It's also very serious and life-threatening. The more you know about bipolar disorder and how it affects you, the better you can manage and overcome the illness.

This chronic illness is best described as a mood disorder. It causes unusual and dramatic shifts in mood, energy, and the ability to think clearly. The mood of someone who is bipolar rotates between polar opposites: at one end of the spectrum are the highs (mania) and at the other end are the lows (depression). The most identifiable bipolar symptoms are these polar mood swings, each of which can last anywhere from days to weeks (WebMD, 2019).

Bipolar disorder can look very different in each person. The symptoms vary widely in their pattern, severity, and frequency. However, bipolar disorder can also be somewhat predictable. For each person, the disorder tends to follow a pattern or can have some consistency. Within the broad groupings of manic and depressive symptoms, each person will have their own markers, or unique expressions of the illness that help to define their specific brand of bipolar disorder. For example, you may notice racing speech and thoughts, prolonged periods of irritability or anger, decreased need for sleep, or delusions of grandeur (HelpGuide, 2020). Recognizing that you are having similar symptoms to ones you experienced during past bipolar episodes can be a huge advantage if you are able to take evasive action sooner rather than later.

As you become familiar with your illness, you can learn your own unique patterns of behavior. If you learn to recognize these signs and seek effective and timely care, you can often prevent additional episodes. Recognizing and naming your typical bipolar symptoms is the first important step to understanding and beginning to take control over your bipolar disease.

Select your Weapons

For those of us who are bipolar, it is important to understand that we are facing a highly complex situation, and we can't hope to change it until we arm ourselves with the necessary psychological and intellectual capacity.

The weapons you select to include in your arsenal can be thought of as strategies, techniques, tactics, and knowledge you can deploy as needed to battle the enemy, your bipolar disorder. Choose your weapons based on the advice of the experts in the medical community, knowledge of the illness from past experiences, and the specific challenges that you currently face.

The nine weapons I selected to include in my battle plan for fighting the war against bipolar disorder are shown in the following figure:

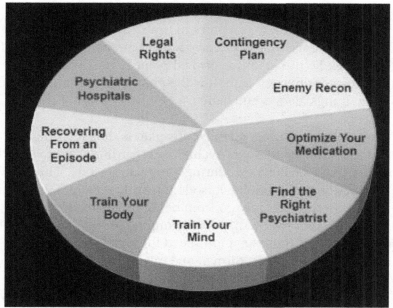

WEAPONS IN MY BIPOLAR BATTLE PLAN

My Bipolar Battle Plan

<u>Weapon 1: Contingency Plan</u>

"Every military disaster can be explained in two words: too late."

–Douglas MacArthur

The contingency plan, explained in Chapter 4, is one of the most important weapons of the overall battle plan. The purpose of the contingency plan is to keep you alive, out of the hospital, and out of jail when you are having a bipolar episode. It is the last line of defense to keep a manic episode from skyrocketing out of control or a depressive episode from plummeting to disaster.

In my experience, there is a point in time during either a manic or depressive episode when I have a lucid moment and realize I need to seek help. This is the critical point in time when I must launch my contingency plan. It is the point of no return—if I do nothing, things always end badly.

An important part of my contingency plan is the prearranged agreement I made with my psychiatrist regarding what to do if I start going off the deep end during a bipolar episode. There have been times during a bipolar episode, or while recovering from an episode, where I suddenly go from being okay to feeling like swallowing all of my medications, jumping off of a bridge while taking a walk, or running at top speed through a grocery store. It is as if a switch has been thrown and my brain has been invaded by a crazy man who hijacked my thoughts. I have to fight with all my might to avoid disaster. When I talked this over with my psychiatrist, he told me to carry a 400 mg tablet of Seroquel (one of my medications) in my pocket, and take it immediately if I start having these feelings.

Another critical part of my contingency plan was to assemble a team of people who I can call for help when my bipolar illness starts to get the best of me. My team consists of my psychiatrist, my daughter Rachel, and my uncle Bud. They all know my history and struggles with bipolar disorder and I trust them with my life.

Recommendations:

1. Always remember there are help lines with people on call at all times. Some examples include the National Suicide Prevention Lifeline (1-800-273-8255), the Mental Health Hot Line (1-844-549-4266), and the Substance Abuse and Mental Health Helpline (1-800-662-4357). There is also the Crisis Text Line (Text 'HOME'

to 741741). Most importantly, if you are in trouble and your life is on the line, dial 911.

2. There is a form at the end of the book that can be used to put your contingency plan in writing if you choose to do so.

3. Keep in mind that even a badass needs to be rescued every once in a while!

Weapon 2: Enemy Reconnaissance

The more knowledge and understanding you have of bipolar disorder, the better you can control your illness. It is important to educate yourself on all aspects of bipolar disorder, just like you would do if you were going to have a major operation such as brain surgery or kidney replacement. Study the subject as if you are getting a Master's degree in Bipolar Disorder. Never stop learning.

Chapter 5 provides a detailed understanding of the true nature of the enemy, bipolar disorder. This includes the definitions of five types of bipolar disorder, as well as descriptions of mania, hypomania, depression, mixed-episode, seasonal pattern, bipolar episode triggers, and sleep disturbances. Also included are a number of facts and statistics about bipolar disorder, the causes of bipolar disorder, and current research that is underway on bipolar disorder.

Weapon 3: Optimize Your Medication

Learning how to determine the best medications to treat your bipolar illness is imperative, and can be one of your most powerful weapons in fighting the war against bipolar disorder. Your psychiatrist will prescribe your medications, but you are the only one who can tell if they are working effectively. You must become an expert at treating your own disease.

Chapter 6 explains how to determine the best medications and corresponding dosages to effectively battle your bipolar illness and achieve optimal mental and physical health. This includes being your own mental detector, researching your medications, dialing-in your medications, ramping up and ramping down your medications, knowing the possible side effects of each of your medications, and understanding the reasons why people stop taking their medications.

It is your job to push the limits of your medications in order to find the sweet spot where you are mentally sharp and focused, have plenty of get up and go, a positive attitude, no bipolar symptoms, and are happy with yourself and your life.

Recommendations:

1. It can be extremely detrimental to stop taking your medications, especially all at the same time. Two of my bipolar episodes escalated out of control when I stopped taking my medications. I ended up in the psychiatric hospital on both occasions.

2. Keep a close eye on your medications and don't let yourself run out or forget them if you go on a trip. It is easy to do and has happened to me more than once. Going without my medications for even a couple of days will drastically mess with my mind. Also, I keep an extra set of daily medications in my vehicle in case I forget to take my pills in the morning.

3. If you don't have prescription insurance coverage, or even if you do, there are huge savings to be had by using GoodRx (www.goodrx.com). For example, I filled a prescription for 30 days of 400 mg tablets of Seroquel. Since I don't have prescription insurance it was going to

cost $370.00. Fortunately, using GoodRx, it only cost me $17.00 for the same prescription.

Weapon 4: Choose the Right Psychiatrist

Finding a psychiatrist who you trust to treat your bipolar disease and keep you healthy, alive, and out of the hospital is essential. The skills, abilities, and competence of your psychiatrist to repair, tune up, and maintain your mind can be likened to that of an auto mechanic who is the only person you trust to work on your car.

Chapter 7 discusses how to rate a psychiatrist, how to get the most out of appointments with your psychiatrist, when you should consider getting a new psychiatrist, and also provides pointers on how to find a new psychiatrist.

Remember, you are the customer paying a professional for their services. If your current psychiatrist isn't meeting your expectations, find someone who is better suited for your needs.

Weapon 5: Train Your Mind

Your mind is your most powerful weapon. Your thoughts are the only thing over which you can exert complete control. What you think and believe becomes a reality and rules your life. However, for those of us who are bipolar, it is a paradox that we must use our mind to fight a disease that at times has the power to take control of it.

Chapter 8 includes strategies and techniques you can use to strengthen your mind, increase emotional well-being, decrease stress, and bring you happiness and joy. Three of my favorite strategies are: "The Path With Heart," "Always Do Your Best," and "Self-Importance Is Your Greatest Enemy."

Recommendations:

1. Operate on the premise that it takes the same amount of work to make yourself strong as to make yourself miserable. It is in your power.

2. One technique I use on a daily basis that is making a positive difference is paying close attention to my thoughts. If I notice I am thinking in a negative way, ruminating over past events, or worrying about what people think of me, I say out loud my keyword "Noise", and change my train of thought to something more productive. My psychiatrist recommended I try this idea and it has served me well in my experiences.

Weapon 6: Train Your Body

If you take care of your body, your body will in turn take care of you. Your mind and body are a unit; being good to your body benefits your mind. Taking care of your body will help stabilize your mood and maximize your energy for the battles ahead.

Chapter 9 includes a number of things you can do to improve your physical health and turn your body into a weapon.

Recommendations:

1. For those of us who are bipolar it is CRUCIAL to get enough sleep. Lack of sleep is one of the strongest triggers of a bipolar episode (Kvarnstorm, 2018). If you are having trouble sleeping, get a sleep aid from your psychiatrist. You can also try taking Melatonin or ZzzQuil which is available over the counter. Meditation and herbal tea may also help.

2. Avoid getting sick. If someone around you is sick (coughing, fever, etc.), immediately distance yourself

from them, even if you have to make a disturbance, like moving to new seat during a sermon in church. Do your best not to let them infect you, because life is way too short to be sick.

May 1, 2020: I wrote the paragraph above in December 2019, before the advent of the Corona Virus (COVID 19) pandemic currently spreading across the globe. Now it is more important than ever to heed this advice. In fact, it could be a matter of life or death. As of today there have been 3,300,000 confirmed cases of COVID 19 worldwide, resulting in 235,000 deaths and 1,040,000 recoveries from the epidemic. The United States is the country which has been hit the hardest by COVID 19, with 1,130,000 confirmed cases, resulting in 65,253 deaths and 137,000 recoveries. Scientists are scrambling to find a vaccine as the virus continues to wreak havoc around the world.

3. Making love will keep you energized and can be one of the best therapeutic agents for maintaining good health.

4. If you drink or do drugs, evaluate whether they are keeping you from being your best self. I'm not preaching here, believe me—I can relate. I used marijuana for quite a few years and have finally been able to stop smoking it altogether. Alcohol, pot, or other drugs can trigger an episode if you aren't careful, so treat them with respect. As an alternative to self-medicating with drugs and alcohol, learn to use bipolar medications to your advantage instead. Bipolar medications are very powerful pharmaceutical drugs and if used intelligently can work wonders.

Weapon 7: Recovering from a Bipolar Episode

By definition, a bipolar episode never ends well, unacceptable things have happened, your mind has deceived you, and you crashed and burned. Now you are left to pick up the pieces, regain your balance, and try to get back on an even keel.

Chapter 10 provides a number of actions you can take that will help you deal with the aftermath of a bipolar episode and speed up the time it takes for you to recover. These actions include working closely with your psychiatrist regarding medications, eliminating stress, attending bipolar support group meetings, using coping techniques, forgiving yourself, setting goals, reaching out for face-to-face connection, getting therapy, educating yourself about bipolar disorder, surrounding yourself with people you can depend on, and making a plan to keep from having future episodes.

Recommendation:

The last thing I wanted to do after being released from the hospital was attend a support group. But after a few weeks of attending support group meetings I realized that no matter how I felt before the meetings and no matter what was discussed during them, I always left feeling better.

The wonder of working with a collective is that you get to learn from everyone within it. Often the best lessons came from those who are struggling the most. Because I had the chance to learn lessons vicariously through members of my support group, I have been able to avoid a great deal of suffering and heartache.

Do an online search to find a bipolar support group in your area, or an online support group. Here are a couple websites that could be helpful:

Depression Bipolar Support Alliance:
https://www.dbsalliance.org/support/

The 7 Best Online Bipolar Disorder Support Groups of 2020:

https://www.verywellmind.com/best-online-bipolar-disorder-support-groups-4802211

Weapon 8: What you Need to Know about Psychiatric Hospitals

Hopefully, you will never have to spend time in a psychiatric hospital. However, if you do, knowing what to expect is invaluable in speeding up your recovery and shortening your hospital stay.

Chapter 11 discusses reasons why you should consider checking yourself into a psychiatric hospital, explains the difference between voluntary committal and involuntary commitment, emphasizes the importance of going with the flow, and describes what it is like to be a patient in a psychiatric hospital. Also included are tips for speeding up your recovery time when you are in the hospital.

Weapon 9: Legal Rights

If you have bipolar disorder there are certain legal issues that may arise related to your condition, including job discrimination, consent to treatment issues, and trouble with the law.

Chapter 12 explains:

- Your legal rights as an employee based upon the Americans with Disabilities Act.

- The laws governing involuntary commitment.

- Your legal rights as a patient in a psychiatric hospital.

- Your legal rights if you are incarcerated.

- Whether you can be forced to take medication.

- The process of getting discharged from a psychiatric hospital.

- The benefits of having a Psychiatric Advance Directive.

Bipolar Warrior Training

"There is no such thing as tough; there's trained and there's untrained."

—Denzel Washington, Man on Fire

Now that you have selected your weapons for fighting the war against bipolar disorder, it is time to begin your training. Your objective is to become skillful in the use of each weapon and to master the fundamental technical and tactical skills necessary for warfare. This includes conditioning your mind and body. Conditioning is not only used for the purpose of conditioning for something, but it is also used for the purpose of conditioning against something.

For example, let's assume you are training yourself on using the weapon "Optimize your Medication". Firstly, break your training into steps. The first logical step would be to educate yourself on each medication you are taking, or thinking about taking, by using internet research, reading books, asking your psychiatrist questions, and studying Chapter 6 of this book. Then answer the following questions:

1. How will I know if the medicine is working?

2. What are the expected results or pros of the medicine?

3. What are the side effects and risks or cons of the medicine?

4. What is the target dosage and therapeutic range for this medication?

5. What time of day should I take the medicine?

6. Are there any foods or other substances I will need to avoid?

7. How will this drug interact with my other prescriptions?

Additional steps in your training would be to gain proficiency in rating your medications, ramping up and ramping down a medicine, dialing-in the perfect medication cocktail, as well as educating yourself on the reasons why people stop taking their medicine.

Attributes of the Bipolar Warrior

"The hardest thing in the world is to assume the mood of a warrior. It is of no use to be sad and complain and feel justified in doing so, believing that someone is always doing something to us. Nobody is doing anything to anybody, much less to a warrior."

—Carlos Castaneda

Warcraft of all types must be mastered. Developing expertise and proficiency in fighting the war against bipolar disorder is paramount for everyone with this sometimes devastating illness. I am giving you a call to arms to become a bipolar warrior. Fight, claw and scratch with all of your strength, courage, and willpower to overcome the bipolar beast that invades your mind and wants to destroy you. This is the most difficult and important undertaking you will ever face! No one deserves a negative kind of life and I am passionate in my belief that it should not happen to you or to anyone else.

Ingrain this list of attributes of a bipolar warrior into your mind and incorporate them into your daily routines in order to successfully fight and win the war against bipolar disorder.

A Warrior:

- Knows that this is a battle for their life.

- Understands the will to conquer is the first condition of victory.

- Never accepts the unacceptable.

- Makes a plan to defeat the enemy.

- Knows that no plan survives first contact with the enemy.

- Knows that wars are won on strategy, not impulse.

- Knows that until they understand exactly what is going on and how to stop it, the most important weapon in their arsenal is reason.

- Remains calm and in control at all times.

- Knows that every minute lost in war can be the cause of defeat.

- Makes up their mind to overcome struggles and challenges.

- Adopts the mindset of a warrior every morning when they wake up.

- Always does their best.

- Prepares to battle.

- Knows they are in a war with the parasite in their mind.

- Fights with all their might.

- Makes a plan and sticks to it.

- Takes action to further their plan on a daily basis.

- Focuses on what they can control.

- Knows that once they face down the enemy, they are able to accommodate, or even work with them.

- Rolls with the punches.

- Knows their strengths and weaknesses.

- Avoids being taken by surprise.

- Knows that even a badass needs rescued every once in a while.

- Practices vigilance.

- Learns as much as possible because information is power.

- Voices and directs daily intentions.

- Respects their enemies.

- Knows that sometimes they have to change things up.

- Trains their mind.

- Trains their body.

- Shores up their defenses wherever needed.

- Eats healthy and stays hydrated.

Precious moments have already been snatched from your life by the enemy, and it will only try to steal more—if you allow it. Make the decision to win the war against bipolar disorder **NO MATTER WHAT**. Victory means living a productive, happy life—and making your dreams come true!

"A wise man once told me to always have a contingency plan."
—Abraham Lincoln, 16th President of the United States
Believed to have had Bipolar Disorder

Chapter 4

Make A Contingency Plan

The purpose of the contingency plan is to keep you alive, out of the hospital, and out of jail when you are having a bipolar episode. It is the last line of defense to keep a manic episode from skyrocketing out of control or a depressive episode from plummeting to disaster.

When it becomes hard to ignore your manic or depressive symptoms, you must take immediate action. Bipolar episodes escalate like wildfire, so a rapid response is **EVERYTHING**. The stakes are too high to allow yourself to slide into a bipolar episode of disastrous proportions.

This chapter outlines how to create a contingency plan, the role your psychiatrist plays in it, when to put your contingency plan into action, and lists both manic and depression early warning signs. Equally important is creating a team that is aware of your contingency plan, should you need their help when it is critical. My story in Chapter 1, "The Hospital Roof," drives home how important it is to have a contingency plan in place and ready to execute. In retrospect, it would have been wise if not critical for me to execute my contingency plan the moment I chose not to take my prescribed medications.

There is a form at the end of the book that can be used to put your contingency plan in writing if you choose to do so.

Jane's Contingency Plan

Jane relates how she created her contingency plan and shared it with her team:

I asked my psychiatrist whether I could call her at 2:00 a.m. if I was having bipolar symptoms and needed help. She said, "Yes, absolutely, anytime twenty-four/seven. If I am not available then another doctor in my practice will be on call." We discussed what steps to take if I start to have an episode. She told me one thing I could do immediately was adjust my medication. I am currently taking 300 milligrams of Depakote and 900 milligrams of Lithium in the morning, and 400 milligrams of Seroquel at bedtime. She told me if I notice bipolar symptoms to increase my dosage of Seroquel to 600 milligrams for several days. She also told me to carry Seroquel with me and if my symptoms became severe to take a pill immediately, even if I have to chew it.

Another thing I did was ask two people I trust implicitly to be part of my contingency plan. I asked my sister, an ex-alcoholic, whom I am very close with. She knows how to deal with mental adversity and has been sober for five years. I also asked my best friend, Liz. They are both aware of my disease and told me to call day or night if I need help. Finally, I put my contingency plan in writing and gave copies to my sister, Liz, and my psychiatrist.

This is Jane's contingency plan:

- Ensure I am getting sufficient sleep. If not, I will call my doctor and request a sleep aid.

- Call my psychiatrist and make an appointment to see her ASAP or talk to her on the phone.

- Adjust my medication dosage(s) per the pre-arranged plan I made with my psychiatrist.

- Call the people I recruited to be part of my contingency plan.

- Distance myself from my loved ones if I feel agitated, violent, or out of control so they are safe.

- Check myself into the hospital if things get bad enough.

- Remove myself from stressful situations.

- Start taking my medications if I am not currently taking them.

- Stop drinking alcohol and doing drugs.

- Exercise and get fresh air every day.

- Stay hydrated.

- Take vitamins and eat healthy.

The Role of Your Psychiatrist

The most important duties of your psychiatrist are to keep you from having a bipolar episode and to be there for you in your time of crisis. This is why they get paid the big bucks. You must be able to count on your psychiatrist to help you immediately, day or night, if you contact them for help. This means talking to you on the phone or seeing you in person. If they are not reachable, then another on-call doctor must be available twenty-four/seven. If you think you need help, do not hesitate! Call your psychiatrist immediately.

When to Launch Your Contingency Plan

Monitoring yourself for out-of-the-ordinary moods, thoughts, and feelings is a must, rather than an option, for managing your bipolar illness. If you notice symptoms that persist for several days, it is a warning siren that you had better get a handle on what is going on—pronto! Your body and mind are giving you clues that all is not well and you need to take immediate action by talking to your psychiatrist, increasing your medication per the prearranged agreement with your psychiatrist, or talking to your team. If things seem to be getting worse, rather than better, launch your contingency plan before the episode gains steam.

Gary tells about using his contingency plan to keep from going off the deep end:

> I began going manic this past September when the leaves were changing. Fall is historically when my episodes rear their ugly head. My episodes ramp up slowly and unnoticeably, and I start getting really happy, busy, horny, and emotionally intense. I really love these periods in my life, and it's hard to believe anything out of the ordinary is happening.
>
> Then suddenly, I got to the point where I became psychotic. This time I was convinced I was being followed by some Mexicans who were part of a drug cartel and wanted to kill me. I started taking evasive tactics like making sure I wasn't being followed so they wouldn't discover where I lived. I began staying up all night holding a shotgun because I was afraid I was going to be attacked. One morning, I was lucid enough to recognize I needed help and called my friend Chris, who previously had agreed to be part of my contingency plan. He convinced me to call my psychiatrist. My doctor prescribed a stronger medicine, and

I was able to calm down and fortunately rid myself of psychotic thoughts in a few days without having to go to the hospital.

A list of early warning signs for both mania and depression follows. These may indicate the onset of a manic or depressive bipolar episode.

___

Mania Early Warning Signs

- Similar pattern of symptoms from previous episodes

- Heightened mood, exaggerated optimism, and overvalued self-confidence

- Sleep disturbances

- Suicidal thoughts

- Inflated sense of self-importance

- Increased physical and mental activity and energy

- Excessive irritability and aggressive behavior

- Racing speech and thoughts

- Irrational ideas

- Impulsiveness, poor judgment, and distractibility

- Grandiose delusions and hallucinations, such as a direct connection to God

- Increased sex drive

- Compulsion to talk incessantly, unusually sociable

- Jumping from one thought to another or project to project

- Aggressive or fast driving

- Impulsive purchases

- Reckless behavior, such as spending sprees, sexual indiscretions, or alcohol and drug abuse

- Increased interest in risk-taking activities like gambling

- Feeling bulletproof or endowed with special powers or qualities

- Impatience or frustration with the slowness of others

- Paranoia

- Hallucinations

- Argumentative, picking fights (Purse, 2020)

Depression Early Warning Signs

- Similar pattern of symptoms from previous episodes

- Sleep disturbances

- Suicidal thoughts

- Abandoning activities you usually enjoy

- Not answering your phone or replying to emails or texts

- Continually having negative thoughts

- Prolonged sadness or unexplained crying spells

- Loss of energy

- Changes in appetite

- Paying less attention to personal appearance, hygiene, and grooming

- Social withdrawal and isolation

- Increased feelings of worry and anxiety

- Feelings of guilt or hopelessness

- Little interest in sex

- Inability to concentrate or make decisions

- Unexplained aches or pains

- Slowed and difficultly thinking

- Paranoia

- Hallucinations

- Self-Loathing (Smith, 2019)

"At sometimes in our lives a devil dwells within us, causes heartbreak, confusion, and troubles, then dies."
—Theodore Roosevelt, 26th President of the United States
Believed to Have Had Bipolar Disorder

Chapter 5

Enemy Reconnaissance

T here is no cure for bipolar disorder, only treatment and management (Burgess, 2019). The more knowledge you have of the illness, the better chance you have to win the war against bipolar disorder.

This Murderous Cauldron

"In a rage I pulled the bathroom lamp off the wall. I see in the mirror blood running down my arms, collecting into the tight ribbing of my beautiful, erotic negligee, only an hour ago used in passion of an altogether different and wonderful kind. I can't help it, I chant to myself, but I can't say it; the words won't come out, and the thoughts are going by far too fast. I bang my head over and over against the door. God, make it stop, I can't stand it. I know I'm insane again. I can't think, I can't calm this murderous cauldron, my grand ideas of an hour ago seem absurd and pathetic, my life is in ruins, and worse still—ruinous; my body is uninhabitable. It is raging and weeping and full of destruction and wild energy gone amok. In the mirror I see a creature I don't know but must live and share my mind with. I understand why Jekyll killed himself before Hyde had taken over completely, I took a massive overdose of Lithium with no regrets."

The above excerpt from the book *An Unquiet Mind* by Kay Jamison illustrates the changes in mood that intensify as a bipolar episode progresses. Kay goes from having "grand ideas" to an hour later feeling like she is "insane again" and her body is "uninhabitable." When a bipolar episode has progressed to this state there is nothing that can stop you from crashing and burning except getting help. Fortunately, Kay was rescued from this suicide attempt and continues her career as a professor of psychiatry at the Johns Hopkins University School of Medicine, as well as being a renowned author of books on mental illness. I highly recommend her national bestseller *An Unquiet Mind.*

What Is Bipolar Disorder?

Bipolar disorder is a chronic illness that is best described as a mood disorder. This mental illness causes unusual and dramatic shifts in mood, energy, and the ability to think clearly. The mood of someone who is bipolar rotates between polar opposites: at one end of the spectrum are highs (mania) and at the other end are lows (depression). The most identifiable bipolar symptoms are these polar mood swings, each of which can last anywhere from days to weeks. Not everyone's symptoms are the same, and the severity of mania and depression can vary. Some people have "mixed states" in which they feel both mania and depression at the same time (WebMD, 2020).

Bipolar disorder can affect a person's energy level (Legg, 2019), judgment (Gibbons-Gwyn, 2009), memory (MacGill, 2019), sleep patterns (WebMD, 2019), sex drive (Connell, 2019), and self-esteem (Rodriguez, 2012). Bipolar disorder has also been linked to anxiety (Cirino, 2019), substance abuse (Cerullo, 2007), and health problems such as diabetes (Woods, 2015), heart disease (Mcquillan, 2019), migraines (Bledsoe, 2010), and high blood pressure (Nauert, 2018). You may be asking yourself: *What doesn't bipolar disorder affect?*

A common misconception is that people believe themselves to be bipolar due to experiencing the everyday ups and downs of life. The difference in being bipolar is that these feelings are experienced in a much more drastic and dramatic way.

Some people alternate between extreme episodes of mania and depression, but most are depressed more often than they are manic. People with bipolar disorder may also go for long stretches of time without symptoms. However, the condition is usually cyclical, so be prepared for it to worsen and then improve at times. For those of us who live with bipolar disorder, this means accepting that mood swings and episodes of mania or depression will always be a potential challenge for us (WebMD, 2020).

My dad was bipolar in the extreme but never admitted it or took medicine to control it. He would become manic and be high as a kite for several weeks, usually heading to Las Vegas or Atlantic City to gamble heavily. During his manic periods, he was busy managing his bar business, playing poker, attempting to start other businesses, and enjoying life. These periods of mania were essentially the driving force behind his success as an entrepreneur. They also backfired through causing him to gamble large sums of money in careless ways. I remember the positive factors associated with his manic episodes most. He would talk to my sisters and I and become involved with our lives. The times when he was depressed were far worse. He would sit in his La-Z-Boy watching television in his robe, day after day, week after week, uncommunicative and down in the dumps. He kept the bar running, and the only other thing he paid attention to was the television. These depressed periods of time were much longer than the manic periods of time. Having witnessed the detrimental effects of bipolar disorder on my dad, I vowed not to let bipolar disorder disrupt my life as much as it did his.

Five Types of Bipolar Disorder

The medical community has defined five types of bipolar disorder which are used to diagnose people with the illness and determine treatment plans accordingly (Leonard, 2019):

Bipolar 1 Disorder (Mania or a Mixed Episode)

Bipolar I Disorder is the classic manic-depressive form of the illness. This involves manic episodes lasting 7 days or more, or severe mania that requires hospitalization. The person may also experience a major depressive episode that lasts 2 weeks or more. A person does not have to experience this type of episode to receive a bipolar I diagnosis.

Bipolar 2 Disorder (Hypomania and Depression)

This features both mania and depression, but the mania is less severe than in bipolar I, and doctors call it hypomania. A person with bipolar II may experience a major depressive episode preceding or following a manic episode.

Bipolar 3 (Cyclothymic Disorder)

This type includes symptoms of hypomania and depression that last for 2 years or more in adults or 1 year in children. These symptoms do not fit the criteria for wholly manic or depressive episodes.

Bipolar 4 Disorder

In Bipolar 4 Disorder, hypomanic and manic episodes come from taking antidepressant drugs. Doctors prescribe anti-depressant medication to treat other types of mental illness. Unfortunately, antidepressants are known to trigger bipolar disorder in many cases.

Bipolar 5 Disorder

This subtype refers to patients who have a family history of bi-polar disorder but only have symptoms of major depression themselves.

Mania

Remember this rule of thumb if you are experiencing a manic episode: "What goes up must come down." Mania causes people with bipolar illness to climb higher and higher and then crash like a wave rolling into the shore.

When experiencing mania, the bipolar individual is very produc-tive, running around like there is never enough to do. They tend to be really happy and optimistic about life. If a person has ex-treme manic episodes, hallucinations and psychotic symptoms are possible. Psychosis is a state in which a person is unable to tell the difference between reality and non-realistic states of mind. Psychotic symptoms may include hallucinations and false beliefs about having special powers or a special identity—such as believing you are God, have superhuman strength, or have X-ray vision (York, 2017). This can be a neat experience, with the mind offering escape through fantasy, but it is not reality.

During a manic episode, a person might impulsively quit a job, charge up huge amounts on credit cards, or feel rested after sleeping only two hours. Manic symptoms can include minute-to-minute mood swings, rapid speech, grandiosity, impulsive-ness, delusions, the feeling of complete invincibility, and the ab-solute conviction that certain untrue things are true. A manic state can be identified by feelings of extreme euphoria or irrita-bility, agitation, surges of energy, a reduced need for sleep, talk-ativeness, pleasure seeking, and increased risk-taking behavior (York, 2017).

Another symptom of mania called psychomotor agitation manifests itself as unintentional purposeless physical activities that arise from tension and anxiety. Someone may pace around a room, wring their hands, or make more dangerous motions such as ripping, tearing, or chewing at the skin (Burgess, 2016).

Common Symptoms of Mania:

- A long period of feeling overly happy

- Extremely irritable mood, agitation, feeling jumpy or wired

- Talking very fast, jumping from one idea to another, having racing thoughts

- Loss of touch with reality

- Being easily distracted

- Increasing goal-oriented activities, such as starting new projects or businesses

- Being restless

- Reduced need to sleep

- Having an unrealistic belief in One's abilities

- Behaving impulsively and taking part in pleasurable, high-risk behaviors such as spending sprees, impulsive sex, or risky business investments (Mayo Clinic, 2020)

Hypomania

Hypomania is a less severe form of mania. People experiencing hypomania are able to carry on with their day-to-day lives and don't lose touch with reality. Keep in mind that hypomania can escalate to full-blown mania or be followed by a major depressive episode.

Common Symptoms of Hypomania:

- Having a higher or happier mood than usual

- Higher sense of irritability or rude behavior

- Feeling overconfident

- Higher activity or energy levels than usual without a clear cause

- A powerful feeling of physical and mental well-being

- Being much more sociable and talkative than usual (Mayo Clinic, 2020)

Depression

When most people think of bipolar disorder, they think of the manic side. However, depression is the far more common and more damaging of the two poles. In the euphoria of mania, people rarely choose to intentionally harm themselves. In a deep depression, however, self-mutilation and suicidal thoughts and actions are far too common (Dome, 2020).

Depression is a form of reversible brain failure. When someone is depressed, it's like their mental computer processing unit isn't working properly. As a result, focusing on a single idea or task is very difficult. Depression intrudes on their mind and fills it with negative thoughts. When depressed, individuals with bipolar illness may stay in bed all day, feeling that they cannot get going (Dome, 2020).

Depressive symptoms may include dreariness, extreme pessimism, hopelessness, and lack of focus. People who are depressed may feel that their thoughts move slowly, take little pleasure in any activity, feel worthless, and that their lives are meaningless. They often isolate themselves from others. They may begin to overindulge with food and, given their low activity level, gain weight. They may speak or think about suicide or become violent, making emergency care crucial for their safety and others. In addition, psychotic symptoms may occur during severe depressive episodes (WebMD, 2019).

People who are depressed undergo a series of physical and emotional changes. They can experience fatigue, as well as an inability to process information, thereby impairing concentration on work or other tasks. Depression also slows down physical movements, speech, and thought processes (WebMD, 2019).

Common Symptoms of Depression:

- A long period of feeling worried or agitated

- Loss of interest in activities once enjoyed, including sex (low libido)

- Feeling tired or slowed down

- Having problems concentrating, remembering, and making decisions

- Being restless or irritable

- Change in eating, sleeping, or other habits

- Thoughts of death or suicide, or actually attempting suicide (Mayo Clinic, 2020)

Mixed Episode

A mixed episode is when symptoms of depression and mania are experienced at the same time. This can lead to irritability, hostility, and physical aggression. Depending on the severity of the symptoms, patients may be hospitalized for their safety and the safety of those around them. They may need a longer hospital stay and a combination of more than one medication to get well (WebMD, 2020).

Seasonal Pattern

Seasonal pattern describes mood disorders that are triggered by a particular season of the year. For example, someone who tends to become manic during the spring and summer and then returns to a regular mood during the late fall and winter has a seasonal pattern of mania. Alternatively, someone who tends to become depressed during the late fall and winter and then returns to a regular mood during the spring and summer has a seasonal pattern of depression (Hook, 2015). "The fall/winter depression pattern is more common than the spring / summer pattern. Suicide is far more common in March, April and May, probably due to changes in light" (Martin, 2006).

Each bipolar individual has their own specific footprint of both mania and depression. Pay attention to your moods during different seasons of the year and determine if you have a seasonal mood pattern. If so, you can adjust your treatment plan accordingly.

Bipolar Episode Triggers

Triggers are outside events that can launch new episodes of mania or depression or cause existing bipolar symptoms to worsen (Kvarnstorm, 2018). Triggers are the main environmental causes of mood swings and need to be monitored and eliminated as much as possible. One of the best ways to prevent future episodes is to identify and avoid the specific triggers that ignite your bipolar symptoms. Lack of sleep, going off of your medications, alcohol and drugs, and major stress are some of the top triggers that set off a bipolar episode (Vann, 2017).

Scott tells about two bipolar triggers he has learned to avoid:

> *I used to get stressed out whenever I traveled back to Indiana for family gatherings at my mom and dad's. A couple of years ago, I came back home from visiting my parents over the Christmas holidays and ended up having a bipolar episode and sinking into depression for a couple of months. I figured out that the two biggest stress factors for me during these visits are being around a large group of people and not having my own place to retreat. I still go home to visit but not during the holidays. I go when I can visit with just a few people at a time. Also, I stay in a hotel instead of staying at my mom and dad's place. Since I made these two changes, my last two visits have been enjoyable.*

For each of us, our stressors and triggers are different. Identifying the triggers that may set you off can help you to avoid an episode. Once you identify your personal triggers, you can work on recognizing them as they occur and handle them more effectively.

Common triggers of bipolar episodes:

- Sleep irregularities

- Financial problems

- Increase in stress

- Isolation

- Stop taking medications

- Alcohol or drug abuse

- Side effects from medications

- Change of seasons

- Forgetting to take medicine

- Conflict with others

- New relationships

- Lack of exercise

- Birth of a child

- Travel and jet lag

- Feelings of loneliness and despair

- Non-supportive family or friends

- Relationship problems and breakups

- Change in smoking habits

- A death in the family

- Stress at work

- Promotion at work

- A vacation

- Change in environment

- Moving residences

- Poor nutrition

- Physical illness

- Loss of employment

- Taking on more than you can handle

- Changing jobs

- Thyroid malfunction (Vann, 2017)

Sleep Disturbances

Getting sufficient sleep is CRUCIAL if you are bipolar. Sleep disturbances are a key symptom of both mania and depression and an excellent early warning sign of a mood change (WebMD, 2019). Your ability to get a good night's rest is highly influenced by the circadian system, which is the body's twenty-four hour internal biological clock. The circadian rhythm of your body determines when you need sleep, and when you need to wake. It is through this rhythm that your body knows when to start and stop certain chemicals in your brain. To put it simply, regulated sleep stabilizes the brain chemicals that control emotions. Maintaining a consistent sleep schedule and wake time can help you avoid nighttime sleeplessness or daytime exhaustion, which can increase the risk of new episodes of mania or depression (Alloy, 2017).

Regulating sleep is often one of the best ways to balance moods and the circadian system. When you go to sleep easily, sleep and dream deeply, and then wake up refreshed on a set schedule every day, you're experiencing regulated sleep.

Unfortunately, maintaining a regular sleep schedule is not always as easy as it sounds, especially if your neighbors, family, roommates, schedule, lifestyle, or sleeping arrangements do not cooperate. The more you upset the natural circadian rhythm by working odd hours, staying out late and partying, ignoring what you put into your body, or watching upsetting television before bedtime, the less likely you are to find stability. You may need to change some of these behaviors in order to kick your circadian rhythm into gear so that you can sleep more soundly and therefore give your brain and your body time to recharge. Sticking to a sleep routine, winding down with pre-bedtime rituals, reducing caffeine intake, and getting your family or roommates to cooperate can prove to be very helpful.

Common contributors to unregulated sleep include:

- Shift work or work that upsets your sleep patterns such as an ever-changing schedule

- Stress

- Drugs and alcohol

- Caffeine

- Travel to different time zones

- Anything new: new baby, new job, new city, etc.

- Frisky bed partner (might be worth losing some sleep ☺)

- Bright light before bed (Harvey, 2015)

Learn to avoid the events and circumstances that may trigger you to have a bipolar episode. If something triggers you, promptly launch your contingency plan.

Bipolar Disorder Is Somewhat Predictable

What is your bipolar modus operandi? Bipolar disorder can look very different in each person. The symptoms vary widely in their pattern, severity, and frequency. Some people are more prone to either mania or depression, while others alternate equally between the two poles. Some have frequent mood disruptions, while others experience only a few over a lifetime (HelpGuide, 2020).

However, bipolar disorder can be somewhat predictable. For each person, the disorder tends to follow a pattern. It surprisingly has some consistency. Within the broad groupings of manic and depressive symptoms, each person has their own markers or unique expressions of the illness that help to define that person's specific brand of bipolar disorder. For example, you may notice racing speech and thoughts, prolonged periods of irritability or anger, decreased need for sleep, or delusions of grandeur (HelpGuide, 2020). Recognizing that you are having similar symptoms to ones you experienced during past bipolar episodes can be a huge advantage if you are able to take evasive action sooner rather than later.

As you become familiar with your illness, you can learn to recognize your own unique patterns of behavior. If you learn to self-recognize these recurring signs and seek effective and timely care, you can often prevent additional episodes. Recognizing and naming your typical bipolar episode symptoms is an important first step to understanding and taking control of your bipolar disease.

Each of the five bipolar individuals I interviewed for this book reported that their bipolar episodes had similar characteristics. John, Scott, and Ruth's episodes start with mania, whereas Gary and Jane's episodes start with depression. Also, the symptoms they experienced were comparable between episodes. This applies to my bipolar episodes as well. John and Scott describe the similarities between their episodes below.

John describes the symptoms he experienced at the onset of his past bipolar episodes:

> *At the beginning of my bipolar episodes, I become more expansive, feel more in tune with other people, and don't sleep as much. A common symptom of mine is attributing hidden meanings to things that happen and what people say, even if I just overhear conversations. Another symptom I experience is hearing God talking directly to me telling me what to do. These days I keep tabs on what I am thinking and monitor my mood on a regular basis. If I notice any of these symptoms, I know I better do something fast because an episode is brewing.*

Scott has also learned to monitor himself closely for symptoms based on previous episodes:

> *My bipolar episodes always begin on the manic side. There is a critical juncture in time where I realize that I am having off-the-wall thoughts, or other symptoms, and I know I need help. At this point in time, I usually make an attempt to get help by calling my psychiatrist. However, if I don't talk to him or see him that day, it's too late, game over. I be-*

come more and more obstinate. My mania grows exponentially and gathers steam like a runaway freight train without any brakes.

Bipolar Disorder Facts and Statistics

The numbers and statistics presented here are representative of research from a variety of sources, including both online and published material.

The list below characterizes the true nature of bipolar illness:

- Up to 20 percent of people with bipolar disorder end their life by suicide, and 20-60 percent of them attempt suicide at least once in their lifetime (Dome, 2019).

- More than 40 percent of people with bipolar disorder struggle with alcohol and drug abuse (Cerullo, 2007).

- Bipolar disorder affects approximately 5.7 million American adults, or about 2.6 percent of the US population age eighteen and older in a given year (Kessler, 2005).

- Bipolar disorder results in 9.2 years reduction in expected life span (National Institute of Mental Health, 2019).

- Approximately 25 percent of bipolar individuals are obese (McElroy. 2002).

- People with bipolar disorder are three times more likely to develop diabetes than members of the general population (Thompson, 2010).

- Three of the top methods of bipolar suicide are guns, suffocation (hanging), and poisoning (overdose) (Mariant, 2012).

- Approximately 15 percent of people with bipolar disorder have had a violent episode. Bipolar individuals are prone to agitation that may result in impulsive aggression (as opposed to premeditated aggression) during manic and mixed episodes. However, depressed states, which can involve intense agitation and irritability, also carry a risk of violent behavior (Vann, 2010).

- Bipolar disorder doesn't discriminate by age, race, ethnicity, or social class. It affects as many men as women (Sachs, 2008).

- There are many factors leading to medication non-adherence in psychiatric patients, including lack of insight into having an illness, distress associated with side effects affecting quality of life, lack of family and social support, insufficient information on the disease and treatment, and substance abuse or addiction (Mert, 2015).

- There are no specific blood tests or brain scans to diagnose bipolar disorder (Krans, 2015).

- Bipolar disorder is not curable but there are many treatments and strategies that a person can use to manage their symptoms (Burgess, 2019).

Causes of Bipolar Disorder

The exact cause of bipolar disorder is unknown. It is not clear whether it may lie dormant in the brain and be activated on its own or is triggered by environmental factors such as social circumstances, psychological stress, abuse, significant loss, imbalanced hormones, or traumatic experiences (Mayo Clinic, 2020).

Experts believe bipolar disorder is partly caused by an underlying problem with specific brain circuits and functioning of brain chemicals called neurotransmitters. The brain is made up of billions of nerve cells (neurons) that move a constant stream of information from one to another. Chemical messengers in the brain known as neurotransmitters transmit signals between neurons. Neurotransmitters play a crucial role in emotional health, are involved in brain functions, and also help in the functioning of the human body. The abnormal brain circuits identified in bipolar brains are believed to cause certain neurotransmitters in the brain to be dysfunctional (WebMD, 2019).

Neurotransmitters

Scientists have identified serotonin, dopamine, and norepinephrine as the three prevalent neurotransmitters involved in mood regulation, stress responses, pleasure, reward, and cognitive functions such as concentration, attention, and executive functions. When the levels or density of these neurotransmitters are not at a normal level, the result can be the manifestation of bipolar disorder (WebMD, 2019).

Serotonin is a brain chemical that is connected to several body functions such as wakefulness, sleep, sexual activity, eating, learning, impulsivity, and memory. Any abnormal rise or fall in the serotonin levels of the human brain can lead to mood disorders, which elevate medical conditions such as bipolar disorder (McIntosh, 2018).

Dopamine has consistently been linked with the part of the brain that controls the human pleasure center. This neurotransmitter helps control body movements and patterns of thought, while also regulating how hormones are released. Abnormal dopamine activity in individual's brains may explain the symptoms of bipolar disorder (Newton, 2009).

Norepinephrine plays a role in cognition, mood, emotions, movement, and blood pressure. Imbalance in norepinephrine causes difficulty concentrating, fatigue, anxiety, apathy, and depression (Dutta, 2019).

Research on Bipolar Disorder

Positron Emission Tomography (PET) is a brain-imaging technique that has been used to measure the monoamine density of cells that release the brain chemicals dopamine, serotonin, and norepinephrine (Chugani, 1987). "By performing PET scans in areas of the brain in which monoamine-releasing cells are concentrated, an approximate 30 percent increase in density of these cells was found in the brains of bipolar people even when not having symptoms". The altered brain chemistry due to excessive monoamine cells directly affects cognitive and social functions (Evidence of Brain Chemistry Abnormalities, 2005).

Studies continue to determine which kinds of monoamine cells are involved in producing serotonin and norepinephrine. Those findings could help define specific subtypes of bipolar disorder and aid in the development of medications and drug combinations that target a specific patient's personal brain chemistry to alleviate symptoms.

Magnetic resonance imaging (MRI) technology has been used to view the brains of individuals with bipolar disorder. The results of these studies showed gray-matter abnormalities in various regions of the brain. Gray matter is a major component of the central nervous system, consisting of neuronal cell bodies. "Scientists have found gray matter deficits in the ventromedial prefrontal regions of the bipolar brain (located in the rear of the front part of the brain, inside the cortex and atop the orbits of the eyes), and in the anterior limbic cortices of the brain". The particular brain areas affected with gray-matter deficits impact certain brain functions. The ventromedial prefrontal regions of the brain affect concentration, inhibition, emotions, behavior, and learning, and the anterior limbic cortices affect smell, agitation, emotional control, and memory (Narita, 2011).

By studying the gray matter found in the brains of bipolar and non-bipolar individuals, scientists hope to correlate the volume of gray matter with the duration of bipolar illness and the number of episodes.

Genetic Predisposition

Bipolar disorder has a strong but as-of-yet unknown tie to DNA. There is an overwhelming amount of evidence that bipolar disorder can be inherited. "The evidence for a genetic predisposition to bipolar disorder is so strong that based on studies of twins, an estimated 80 percent of the risk is inherited. If one of your parents or siblings has the disorder, your chances of having bipolar disorder are four to ten times greater than they would be if no one in your family had it". The author concludes that approximately 33 percent of children who have a parent with bipolar disorder will contract the disease (Haycock, 2010).

Gary comments on the possibility that his kids may have inherited bipolar disorder:

Are you kidding me? Having to deal with my bipolar disorder is hard enough without worrying my kids may also have it. I have talked to each of my kids about my illness. They have witnessed how the disease affects me, visited me in the hospital, and have been around me when I was manic or depressed. I pray that none of my children are bipolar with all of my heart!

Scientists are trying to find specific genes that are involved in causing bipolar disorder in hopes of finding genetic markers that will provide knowledge of an individual's risk of developing the disorder. A combination of both genetic research and neuroimaging studies are being pursued to help define both the genetic components of this illness and their relationship with specific brain markers that define a chemical fingerprint of bipolar patients.

The important thing to remember is this—what's inherited in bipolar disorder is not the illness itself but vulnerability. Whether the person does or does not get the illness depends on what is happening in that person's life. Interventions like medications or family interventions that reduce stress and introduce structure to someone who is vulnerable to bipolar illness can be very helpful and may prevent or delay the onset of the illness (Tartakovsky, 2020).

"She's got herself worked out with her meds and she's raring to go!"

(Quote from Husband Michael Douglas)
—Catherine Zeta-Jones, Actress
Diagnosed with Bipolar Disorder

Chapter 6

Optimize Your Medication

"Up there, we gotta push it. That's our job."

Tom Skerritt, Call Sign Viper, Top Gun

This chapter explains how to determine the best medications and corresponding dosages to effectively battle your bipolar illness and achieve optimal mental and physical health.

Like heart disease or diabetes, bipolar disorder is a biological illness (Legg, 2020), (Mayo Clinic, 2020) and most often, medication is required to treat it (Mayo Clinic, 2018). Medication can bring your mania and depression under control and prevent relapses once your mood has stabilized. Bipolar disorder has a number of different symptoms, reflecting difficulties in several different areas or systems of the brain. Different medicines target separate brain functions. You may need medicines to help stabilize your mood, curb manic symptoms, relieve depressive symptoms, help you sleep, manage anxiety, control psychosis, improve information processing, or compensate for side effects (Mayo Clinic, 2020), (University of Texas Health Science Center, 2017), (Clark, 2008), (Hibar D. 2017).

It takes skill, finesse, and guts galore to determine the specific medications that will effectively combat your bipolar disorder. Just as it takes time and practice to learn golf or a new language, learning how to use the powerful pharmaceutical medications to effectively treat your bipolar illness is a skill that improves with experience. It is your job to push the limits of your medications in order to find the sweet spot where you are mentally sharp and focused; have plenty of get up and go; a positive attitude; no bipolar symptoms; and are happy with yourself and your life.

Unfortunately, this process is far from easy. It would be awesome if the first time you are prescribed medication to treat your bipolar illness, the medicine(s) worked wonderfully, suppressed your symptoms, and kept you from having future bipolar episodes. However, this is rarely the case, and it is more likely that adjustments will need to be made to your medications as time goes on. Do not be afraid to take calculated risks in making changes with buy-in from your psychiatrist. You do not want medications to make you feel mediocre; you want them to make you feel great!

Bipolar Heal Thyself

You are the General of your own individual bipolar battle plan. Your psychiatrist will prescribe your medications, but you are the only one who can tell if they are working effectively. You must become an expert at treating your own disease. Live by the motto, *Bipolar Heal Thyself.*

Strive to find the best combination of medicines to treat your illness, just as heart patients or cancer patients search for the right medicines to treat their disease. Learn to monitor yourself closely and keep an eye out for bipolar symptoms. Collaborate with your psychiatrist regarding the medications you are taking. Learn how to rate your medications and tweak the dosages based on how you feel both mentally and physically.

While medication is typically the foundation behind bipolar disorder treatment, therapy and self-help strategies also play important roles. You can help control your bipolar symptoms by exercising regularly, getting enough sleep, eating a heathy diet, monitoring your moods, keeping stress to a minimum, and surrounding yourself with supportive people and influences. Living with bipolar disorder is challenging. With medication, healthy coping skills, and a solid support system you can live fully while managing your symptoms (HelpGuide, 2020).

Scott relates some of the actions he takes to avoid bipolar episodes:

> To help me avoid bipolar episodes, I take my medications, exercise, eat fairly healthy, and take vitamins. I make sure to go out of my house and talk to someone at least once a day, even if it is just at a Starbucks. I also have appointments with my psychiatrist every two months, spend time with my kids and friends, and don't drink alcohol more than once or twice a week.

Become Your Own Mental Detector

Many diseases can be detected by some kind of medical test—for example, blood tests for diabetes and kidney function, or CT scans for brain tumors, but there is no test to specifically detect bipolar disorder. The telltale signs are bipolar symptoms, major mood changes, and bipolar episodes. This is why it is vital that you stay vigilant in monitoring and assessing your own moods and energy levels (Krans, 2017).

The onset of a bipolar episode is not readily apparent. Episodes start slowly, oftentimes unnoticeably, and they pick up speed as the days go on. You must be astute enough to recognize that you are experiencing bipolar symptoms and strong enough to take appropriate action. Because no one else knows your thoughts, feelings, and inherent behavior patterns like you do, it is crucial that you become your own "mental detector."

Monitor your thoughts, moods, and energy levels on a regular basis. Ask yourself the following questions:

1. Have I laughed today?

2. Do I feel like myself?

3. Do I have a good libido?

4. Am I looking forward to something coming up in the future?

5. Did I barely drag through the day?

6. Am I having any psychotic thoughts?

7. Am I possibly displaying depressive or manic behaviors? If so, how can I best explain to my psychiatrist or to a loved one how my behaviors are 'out of the norm?'

As soon as you notice bipolar symptoms, take action ASAP! Allow no delays—there is no time to lose. This may mean launching your contingency plan, making an appointment with your psychiatrist, and increasing your medication per the previously arranged plan with your psychiatrist. Also remember there are people on your side and readily willing to help you in any way, shape, or form, as long as you take the necessary step of opening up to them and sharing the way you feel.

Accept You Need to Take Medication

People with bipolar disorder are often times reluctant to admit there is a problem. It takes most of us more than one bipolar episode before we are convinced that we actually have a mental illness. The more pain, agony, and disruption to our lives that is caused by a bipolar episode, the sooner we are able to become *believers*. It is a landmark event when you accept that you are bipolar and need to take medication to treat your illness. When you accept that medicine is necessary to minimize symptoms and avoid future episodes, you can reallocate the energy you have been expending rejecting the medicine and channel it into finding the medications that work best.

You must be your own judge and jury to determine whether you need to take medication—no one else is in a fitting position to do so. Make the decision based on the ramifications of having another bipolar episode and also on optimizing your health, happiness, and life. You may also want to consider whether trying medications to treat your illness could additionally benefit those around you – the people you love and care for. Sometimes we are apt to make positive life changes when considering others rather than ourselves.

Substitute Medicine for Alcohol and Drugs

An important statistic to keep in mind is that more than 40 percent of bipolar individuals abuse alcohol or drugs (Cerullo, 2007). For many of us, it is in an attempt to self-medicate. Instead of seeking health care, we use drugs or alcohol to mask uncomfortable feelings. There's a cultural bias that makes us think, "I should be able to fix this myself, so I'll use the chemicals that I have available to me to help do that."

BREAKING BIPOLAR • 72

The fact of the matter is that you are using depressants to treat your disease. Numbing or masking serious symptoms will only make it worse.

Do not underestimate the negative effects of alcohol and drugs on your mind and body. Why abuse illegal drugs and alcohol when you have some of the strongest pharmaceutical drugs at your disposal? Take the responsibility to not abuse alcohol or drugs and to go from drinking or partying too much to a manner better suited to benefit your overall sense of well-being. Too much can be detrimental to your mind and body. A wise person knows that the key to anything in life is balance.

Ruth gives the following advice:

> *I love to smoke pot and drink martinis like they are going out of style. My problem is I abuse them. I used to get high as a kite, drink too much, and have a hangover the next day that hurt all day long. I still take a puff off of a joint and drink now and then, but I use them in moderation and don't abuse them. Instead, I use my medications to make me feel good. In fact, I believe my medications give me more mental and physical prowess than many people who are not bipolar. I have been taking the same meds for two years and I know I am at the top of my game.*

Dial-In Your Medications

Dialing-in your medications to the optimal dosage is one of the most valuable skills to master. This is where the rubber meets the road. Most bipolar individuals take more than one medicine at a time, and determining the "medication cocktail" that works best takes time, patience, and skill. It's important to work closely with your psychiatrist and reevaluate your medication regularly, because the perfect dosage may change over time.

Self-reflection, in addition to writing in a journal, can be very helpful to track your mood shifts from day to day.

In order to dial-in the optimal dosages of your medications, you must become proficient at researching the medicine, rating your medications, ramping the medicines up or down as needed, and mixing the perfect medication cocktail.

Research Your Medications

Being aware of the pros and cons of any new medication is very important. Research each medication using online resources, the expertise of your psychiatrist, and talking to other bipolar people who are taking the same medication.

Answer the following questions:

1. How will I know if the medicine is working?

2. What are the expected results (pros) of the medicine?

3. What are the side effects and risks (cons) of the medi-cine?

4. What is the target dosage and therapeutic range for this medication?

5. What time of day should I take the medicine?

6. Are there any foods or other substances I will need to avoid?

7. How will this drug interact with my other medication?

8. Is there someone I trust to help me rate or evaluate the effectiveness of my new medication?

Rate Your Medications

It is very helpful to have a methodology to use to determine if your medicine is dialed-in to the optimum dosage. Answer these questions to rate how well your medication is working:

1. Are you sleeping well?

2. Are your moods generally positive?

3. Does the medicine provide benefits? If so, what are they?

4. Do you have any bipolar symptoms? If symptoms persist, do they seem different or downplayed in any way?

5. How is your energy level?

6. Are you experiencing any side effects?

7. Are you being sociable?

8. Do you feel good physically?

9. Are you thinking clearly and logically?

10. What does your heart and intuition tell you?

11. Do you have sexual awareness and drive?

12. Do you feel stable?

13. Do you feel angry?

14. Do you feel like a robot?

15. Are you overly anxious?

16. Are you depressed?

17. Are you manic?

Journaling your thoughts regarding any of these reflective questions can be quite helpful in determining the effectiveness of any medication. It is uncommon, if not impossible, for any medication to immediately change your life. Be patient!

Ramping Up a Medicine

The beginning stage of dialing-in a medication is the ramp up stage, in which you start with a low dosage and increase it until you reach the "therapeutic range." The therapeutic range is reached when the concentration of the medication in the blood is great enough to provide the required therapeutic response, but small enough to restrict the possibility of side effects (Cooney, 2017). Learning how to ramp up a medicine to the optimum dosage is a skill that must be mastered to treat your bipolar illness effectively.

John describes dialing-in a medication called Lamictal:

> I told my psychiatrist that I wasn't happy with the medications I was taking and asked him if he had any recommendations. He said that several of his patients were having positive results with Lamictal, so I decided to give it a try. My psychiatrist told me his patients take a range of dosage of Lamictal from 200 milligrams to 600 milligrams a day. He warned me that a very serious side effect to watch out for is a rash. He told me if I get a rash to stop taking Lamictal immediately because it could actually kill me! His instructions for ramping up the medicine was to start at 100 milligrams for a week, then advance to 200 milligrams the

next week, and continue increasing by 100 milligrams every week until I judged the medication was working optimally. He instructed me to not go over a dosage of 400 milligrams a day until we talked again. I am currently taking 300 milligrams of Lamictal a day and feel great, have lots of energy, and a positive attitude.

Ramping Down a Medicine

You have to be smart enough to know when you have given a medicine a fair chance and when it is time to try a different choice. It is ultimately your decision because your doctor has no way to fully understand your inner feelings, moods, or thoughts. If the medicine is not working, and you have given it a fair chance, it is time to make a change. Make an appointment with your psychiatrist and tell them what your reasons are for wanting to make a change in your medications. Be as specific as possible about why you think your current medication regimen is not working. If you decide you are going to stop taking a particular medicine, it is a very risky and irresponsible idea to stop taking it all at once. Without ramping down your medications, you run the chance of skyrocketing into mania or cliff diving into depression.

Psychiatric medications are extremely powerful, and it takes your mind time to adjust when you are making changes in the dosage. That is why it is so important to gently and slowly ramp down the dosage of medications. A large number of episodes could be avoided if people weaned themselves off of a medication in a controlled fashion rather than stop taking the medicine all at once. Even if you wean yourself off the medicine slowly, it is undoubtedly still going to be a challenge. Count on some unpleasantness, and be prepared to ride out uncomfortable feelings and sensations until the medicine is out of your system completely.

If one of your medications is not working for you, meet with your psychiatrist as soon as possible to figure out the next step(s) to take. Since that medicine didn't work, talk with your doctor about what other medications they recommend.

The Perfect Medication Cocktail

You may have to try a number of different medicines before you zero in on the right medication cocktail that works best to treat your bipolar illness. Keep in mind that the pharmaceutical-grade medicines used to treat bipolar disorder are extremely powerful and that each medicine has its own effects. Finding the right combination and dosages of medicines to effectively treat your bipolar disorder is a trial-and-error process that will most likely take a while. The perfect medication cocktail is different for every individual. The medications or mixture of medicines your doctor recommends based on experience with other patients, or that you read about being so helpful to someone else with the disorder, may not match your specific needs. To attain peace of mind, optimal brain functioning, good energy levels, and overall well-being, you have to keep experimenting with different medicine combinations and dosages until the results meet or exceed your expectations and criteria.

Just getting by is not good enough; settling for less than happiness is a cop-out. Life is short. The right combination of medicines can make you strong, happy, and whole again. Your heart will know when you have found the Holy Grail of medicines that make you glad you are alive!

As time goes by and you experiment with different medicines, you will become more proficient at dialing-in the medications to the optimum dosages for treating your disease. The biggest thing to remember is not to lose hope. You are working toward a better life, and your diligence and patience will pay off.

If all indications are that the medicine or combination of medications is a go, congratulations! You have successfully dialed-in your medications.

Beware of Side Effects

Any time you start taking a new medication, you must be on the lookout for side effects. A side effect is any unwanted, non-therapeutic effect caused by a drug. Most psychiatric medicines have side effects of one kind or another. Some people are prone to experience side effects from a particular medicine, while others do not experience any side effects at all from the exact same medicine (Mayo Clinic, 2020), (University of Texas Health Science Center, 2017). It is vital to watch out for side effects. Be wary because some side effects are more serious than others. Some side effects can actually kill you! Any psychiatrist worth their salt will inform you of the possible side effects when prescribing a medication. If they don't warn you of the possible side effects of the medicine, then consider getting a new psychiatrist. You can also make a habit of automatically asking your doctor how the medication can negatively change or alter your state of being or for warning signs to look out for.

Side effects lie in wait like a lion stalking its prey until the medicine reaches a certain threshold in your bloodstream. Side effects may happen quickly or may occur several days after you begin taking the medicine, while some may not show up until much later. Take heed because this could be weeks or months after you start taking the medication. Everything may be going along smoothly, and then BAM! Things take a very drastic turn, and not in a good way.

If something is going wrong physically or mentally, always look to one of your medications as the possible culprit. The following examples describe extremely undesirable side effects that two

individuals experienced due to two medicines: Risperdal and
Wellbutrin.

These scenarios should not deter you from the idea of trying one
of these medications since everyone experiences ranging effects.

Gary tells about the side effect he experienced with Risperdal:

> *Gary started taking Risperdal in place of a medicine he had
> been taking named Neurontin because he didn't think it was
> working for him. He started taking 2 milligrams a day of
> Risperdal for two weeks, upped it to 4 milligrams for two
> more weeks, and then increased it to 5 milligrams and sta-
> bilized at this dosage. Risperdal definitely was beneficial.
> He had good energy, concentration, and a positive mental
> attitude, so Gary made the decision to stay on it. Everything
> was going great for eight weeks or so, until one night he
> and his wife started fooling around and he didn't get
> aroused. He and his wife hadn't been getting along so he
> thought that was the cause. This went on for several weeks,
> and Gary didn't attribute it to the medicine since he had
> been taking the same dosage for the last two months. Just
> like any other guy would feel, Gary knew this was serious
> business and not acceptable. He ordered some Viagra over
> the counter from Canada and finally got back into action.
> During his next scheduled visit with his psychiatrist, Gary
> told him what was going on. His doctor pulled out a medi-
> cal reference book about six inches thick and looked up
> Risperdal. He told Gary that the percentage of people who
> suffer the side effect of impotence due to Risperdal is up to
> 13 percent. Gary told his psychiatrist, "I'm going off this
> fucking medicine." Once he stopped taking Risperdal, he no
> longer needed the Viagra.*

Jane tells about the side effect she had with Wellbutrin:

Jane began taking a medicine called Wellbutrin to help treat her bipolar illness. After three days, she began vomiting almost instantaneously, without any warning. She puked inside her car and on her living room rug. She couldn't act quickly enough to stop the car or make it to the bathroom. She thought she had the stomach flu. A couple of days later, still puking out of the blue, she attributed it to the medicine and made an appointment with her psychiatrist. Her doctor told her it was more than likely caused by the Wellbutrin. He said that up to 20 percent of people who take Wellbutrin experience the side effect of nausea. Jane discontinued the medication and thought, "Why didn't this dipshit psychiatrist tell me about the possible side effects?" She decided to find a new psychiatrist.

You may be taking more than one medicine at the same time and are not sure which medicine is causing the side effect. Very likely the side effect is a result of the most recent medicine you added to your regimen or a change (typically an increase) in the dosage of a medication. However, this is not always the case. Take immediate action if something strange or unusual is going on mentally or physically.

Some medicines have side effects that will taper off as your body gets used to the dosage level. For example, you may feel dizzy when you reach a certain dosage, but the dizziness goes away once you take that dosage for a few days. You will have to judge the seriousness of the side effect. If it is tolerable, see whether the side effect subsides after a day or two.

The bottom line is that you must monitor yourself mentally and physically when you are taking any kind of medication. If anything unusual starts happening, immediately call your doctor and get an appointment.

Generic Side Effects of Bipolar Medications

A list of generic side effects to carefully watch out for when taking medication for bipolar disorder includes:

- Agitation

- Anxiety

- Blackouts

- Constipation

- Drowsiness

- Excessive thirst/dry mouth

- Hallucinations

- Headaches

- Increased urination

- Insomnia

- Loss of coordination

- Muscle stiffness/pain

- Nausea/Vomiting

- Rashes or itching

- Sedation

- Sensitivity to the sun

- Sexual dysfunction or low libido

- Stomach pain

- Tremors

- Weight gain/increased appetite

- Weight loss (Huizen, 2019)

Medicine Noncompliance

Caution: The top risk factor for relapse into a bipolar episode is going off your medications (Najafi-Vosough, 2016).

Gary tells about his challenges with bipolar medications:

> I resisted taking medication for a number of years after my first bipolar episode. I would take the meds for a while but a few months later get disgruntled that they were not working and I was wasting my life away. I felt like a robot with no real feelings. There were a couple of episodes that wouldn't have ended so badly except I went off my medicines. My most recent episode began a week after I stopped taking Lithium. I ended up heavily medicated in a psychiatric hospital for several days. I have now accepted I need medication to avoid future bipolar episodes. I have been taking my medications on a daily basis and have not had an episode since.

There are a number of reasons why we who have bipolar disorder stop taking our medication:

- A manic episode begins and our thoughts go wild. We love the highs of being manic.

- We don't think the medication is helping.

- The medicine causes unwanted side effects.

- We plan to start taking the medicine again if we experience any bipolar symptoms.

- We want to be "ourselves."

- We think we are smarter now that we have experienced a bipolar episode and can use our willpower to keep from having another.

In conclusion, when taking medication for your bipolar illness, persistently work with your psychiatrist to dial-in your medications so that you have good mental and physical health, no bipolar symptoms to speak of, and feel like a million bucks. Never give up.

"*No pill can help me deal with the problem of not wanting to take pills; likewise, no amount of psychotherapy alone can prevent my manias and depressions. I need both.*"
—Kay Jamison, Writer, Professor of Psychiatry
Diagnosed with Bipolar Disorder

CHAPTER 7

Choose The Right Psychiatrist

Finding a good psychiatrist is crucial to managing your illness and can be a powerful weapon in the ongoing war against bipolar disorder. A psychiatrist is a medical doctor who works to prevent, diagnose, and treat mental, emotional, and behavioral problems. A psychiatrist's medical training allows them to order medical tests and prescribe medication. Psychiatrists complete four years of medical school plus four years in a psychiatric residency program. Their education requires time spent in classrooms, medical offices, and hospitals—working directly with patients and other medical professionals. These are well-educated people devoted to helping others. But, again, not all psychiatrists have the same mindset.

Choosing a psychiatrist is no easy feat because someone else's "good" may not be good for you. Everyone is different. The best course of action is to research and interview a doctor—just like hiring an employee to work for you. While "good" is different for each person, one thing remains the same: a good psychiatrist is one with whom you are happy. That's all. A good psychiatrist is one who performs to your expectations, whatever those may be.

Trust is by far the most important aspect to consider when choosing a psychiatrist. You are putting your trust in this person with your emotional and physical well-being. One of the most important roles of your psychiatrist is for them or their staff to be available anytime, day or night, in your time of crisis. If you recognize you need help because of your bipolar illness, contact your psychiatrist immediately. Don't put it off until later for any reason. If a receptionist answers your phone call, tell them in no uncertain terms that you need to talk to your psychiatrist today as soon as possible. If it is outside of office hours, call the psychiatrist who is on-call—that is what they are there for.

There are good and bad psychiatrists, just as there are good and bad professionals in any trade or industry. A helpful psychiatrist to one patient may be the wrong fit for another. The skills, abilities, and competence of your psychiatrist to repair, tune up, and maintain your mind can be likened to that of a trusted auto mechanic who is the only person you allow to work on your car. Finding a suitable psychiatrist who is beneficial to you can seem like a long, involved process; however, knowing that this doctor is the one you are trusting to treat your bipolar illness and keep you healthy, sane, and alive, as well as possibly partner with you for a lifetime of well-being, makes it well worth your diligent time and effort.

Rating a Psychiatrist

Here is a list of criteria that will help you find a good psychiatrist to treat your bipolar illness:

- They establish a contingency plan with you and tell you to call day or night if you need help.

- They give you instructions on how to modify your medication in the event of serious bipolar symptoms.

- They are skillful at determining your state of mind and zeroing in on your current problems.

- You feel like you can trust them.

- You value their advice.

- They are easy to talk to, and make you feel comfortable.

- They have several years of experience treating bipolar disorder.

- They have hands-on experience in psychiatric hospitals.

- They promote a whole-life wellness plan.

- They are very knowledgeable about medication.

- They explain the pros and cons of each medicine, including possible side effects.

- They explain how to ramp up each medication to the therapeutic range.

- They are covered by your insurance.

- They won't put up with bullshit.

- They are knowledgeable about new research and methods for treating bipolar disorder.

- They are board certified.

- They answer your questions without judgement.

Getting the Most Out of Appointments

Prior to having an appointment with your psychiatrist, it is smart to prepare in advance what you plan to discuss and accomplish. When the appointment begins, your psychiatrist will try to gauge how you are doing and your state of mind. If you are manic, depressed, experiencing noticeable bipolar symptoms, or side-effects, tell your doctor. Keeping your true thoughts or feelings a secret from your doctor will only harm you in the long run.

After questioning you about your mood and state of mind, your psychiatrist will ascertain what dosage you are taking of each of your medications. Then they will assess your medication regimen and decide, based on your input, whether to make a change in the dosage of one of your current medications, or counsel you in regards to going off a medicine or starting a new one. Before the appointment, decide whether your current medicine regimen is optimizing your potential or you feel that a change is needed. If the medicine is not working, be prepared to state the reasons why. Keeping a log is very helpful. The more specific you can be, the better your doctor can treat your condition. If you feel strongly that you need a change in your medications then stick to your guns.

Ruth relates how she prepared for a recent appointment with her psychiatrist:

> *A few days before my scheduled three month appointment with my doctor, I thought about how things were going in my life. I considered my mental state, energy level, relationships, last time I made love (too long), and how my job and career were going. My conclusion was I was too much of a wimp. I wasn't meeting any guys, although I'm fairly attractive. In general, I wasn't pleased with my personality, I was too laid back and not very sociable. When I met with*

*my doctor, I asked him what changes I could make with my
medications to be more assertive. He told me to decrease
the dosage I was taking of Depakote from 750 mg a day to
400 mg.*

Your psychiatrist is not in charge of what medications you take.
You are! The doctor prescribes medication for you and then will
make modifications based upon your feedback. It is your responsibility to keep making changes to your medications until
you find the perfect medication cocktail for optimum mental and
physical health. It's your life, your brain, and your happiness
that are at stake. Keep working with your psychiatrist to find the
medications that make you whole. Continue making adjustments
to your medications until you are happy with the results.

Here are some typical questions a psychiatrist might ask during
an appointment:

1. How's your mood?

2. Are you having any bipolar symptoms?

3. How are your medications working for you?

4. Are you experiencing any side effects from your medications?

5. Are you sleeping well?

6. How's your energy level?

7. How's your job?

8. How is your sex life?

9. Have you been exercising?

10. Are you eating healthy foods?

11. How are your relationships with your significant other, kids, family, and friends?

The only way for a psychiatrist to help you is for you to be brutally honest with both them and yourself. Tell them about any bipolar symptoms you are having and what you are thinking and feeling. This will help them gauge how your medications are working and determine whether a change is warranted.

When to Get a New Psychiatrist

You will know if you are not happy with your psychiatrist in general. Make sure it's not just because you are in a bad mood that week or have taken offense at something they said. Sometimes it is hard for us to hear things we don't want to listen to so try to be open and give your psychiatrist a chance before giving up. In the same sense, don't continue to stagnate with them if you are not seeing any benefit.

If you decide to move on, don't burn bridges with your current psychiatrist until you have found another psychiatrist who you want to partner with, and is willing to prescribe your medications. This is important because you don't want to be at a disadvantage when interviewing a possible new psychiatrist because you need them to write you prescriptions right away.

Finding a New Psychiatrist

Helpful pointers for finding a new psychiatrist include:

- If you have insurance and want to stay in-network, call your insurance company for a list of names. You may be able to look at reviews from other patients if you search in-network providers online.

- If you know someone who likes their doctor, try to schedule an appointment with that same doctor.

- Call your state psychiatric society and ask for a referral.

- Ask your primary care doctor. They are used to making referrals.

- Ask any psychiatrist. They tend to know one another. If you can get one on the phone, they may give you names without seeing you in person.

- If you're a student, try the school's counseling or health center. The staff may also be able to suggest off-campus referrals.

- Search online and query listservs, LinkedIn, Facebook, and other social media sites. Pick a few out of the heap and research them. The easiest way do this is through websites such as HealthGrades.com, which allows you to find doctors by name, specialty, and location. But what is better is that it provides feedback on the doctors, including a background check, which is excellent information to have before you walk into a psychiatrist's office.

- Once you find a potential psychiatrist, call and make an appointment. For your first appointment, you need to decide what questions to ask the doctor to find out if they are a good fit for you. During the first meeting, the doctor is going to be interviewing you. But remember that you are the client and should be interviewing them as well.

- The questions you ask are about opening a dialogue on issues that matter to you. It's not about judgment as much as it is about exploration. You're testing the waters to see if this is the person you think is most able to help you. Do not be intimidated by them whatsoever just because they are doctors.

Here is a list of questions you may want to ask:

1. How long have you been practicing as a psychiatrist?

2. What percentage of your patients are bipolar?

3. What happens if I have an emergency outside of office hours?

4. Have you ever worked in a psychiatric ward or hospital?

5. How do you decide what medications and dosages to prescribe for your patients?

6. What is your view on psychotherapy?

7. How often do you typically see your patients?

8. How long are appointments?

9. How much does an appointment cost?

10. What is your typical treatment plan for your bipolar patients?

11. What is your view on supplements and alternative medication?

12. Are there any medical conditions that could be causing or exacerbating my mood swings?

It is okay if a doctor doesn't meet your expectations. Not every doctor is for every person, and there's nothing necessarily wrong with either of you. If it doesn't work, it doesn't work. It is like a first date. First dates don't always lead to second dates. If you decide it is not going to be a good match, now is the easiest time to say something simple like, "I don't think we're the best therapeutic match. Can you please provide a referral to someone else?"

Scott describes his search for a psychiatrist:

> *It took me awhile to find a psychiatrist who I felt I could trust to save my life if need be, prescribe the best medicines, and help me overcome my bipolar illness. I met with two psychiatrists and interviewed them to decide if I wanted to hire them. The first one impressed me the most and I have been with her for the past three years episode free.*

Ultimately, at the end of the day it is your life, and who you hire to be your psychiatrist is your choice. Your psychiatrist works for you. They are your employee, and you pay them for their services. You decide whether to hire or fire them.

Psychotherapy

Besides prescribing medication, some psychiatrists provide psychotherapy. If they don't, they can usually refer you to a therapist. Therapy can help people reduce stress levels, regulate moods, and change thinking patterns that may trigger episodes. Also, research has established that using psychotherapy in combination with medication to treat bipolar disorder further reduces both the number of relapses that people experience as well as the severity of those relapses. One of the most important outcomes of therapy is self-awareness. For a person with bipolar disorder, self-awareness may mean realizing different events that are likely to trigger a relapse, and learning to recognize signs and symptoms of the onset of depression or mania (Swartz, 2014), (WebMD, 2020).

In her book *Touched with Fire*, Kay Jamison talks about the benefits of psychotherapy:

> *Psychotherapy, in conjunction with medication, is often essential to healing as well as the prevention of possible recurrences. Drug therapy, which is primary, frees most patients from the severe disruptions of manic and depressive episodes. Psychotherapy can help individuals come to terms with the repercussions of past episodes, take the medications that are necessary to prevent recurrence, and better understand and deal with the often devastating psychological implications and consequences of having manic-depressive illness (Jamison 1994, 17).*

Jane conveys a conversation she had with her psychiatrist who also provides psychotherapy:

> *I told my psychiatrist that I was unsure about my relationship with Murray, who had moved in with me six months ago. We have fun together and great sex, but we fight a lot unless we have a few drinks. My psychiatrist advised me to quit drinking with Murray and see how we get along. It took me a while to cool it on the drinking, but I came across two people I respected who had quit drinking in the last couple of years. Talking with them convinced me to give up drinking for a while because I wanted clarity on my relationship with Murray. After I quit drinking for two months, we decided to split up. Murray said I wasn't fun anymore, and we really didn't have much in common. He moved out and I am much happier.*

Good luck Warrior!

"I can calculate the motion of heavenly bodies, but not the madness of people."
—Isaac Newton, Physicist, Mathematian
Believed to have had Bipolar Disorder

CHAPTER 8

Train Your Mind

"We either make ourselves miserable, or we make ourselves strong. The amount of work is the same."

—Carlos Castaneda

Your mind is your most powerful weapon. Your thoughts are the only thing over which you can exert complete control. What you think and believe becomes a reality and rules your life. However, for those of us who are bipolar, it is a paradox that we must use our mind to fight a disease that at times has the power to take control of it.

Learning strategies and techniques to strengthen your mind will improve brain power, increase emotional well-being, decrease stress, and bring happiness and joy to your life. This chapter includes strategies from several self-help gurus such as Napoleon Hill, Miguel Ruiz, Carlos Castaneda, and others.

The Path With Heart

Anything is one of a million paths. Therefore, a warrior must always keep in mind that a path is only a path; if he feels that he should not follow it, he must not stay with it under any condition. His decision to keep on that path or to leave it must be free of fear or ambition. He must look at every path closely and deliberately. There is a question that a warrior has to ask, mandatorily. Does this path have a heart? A path without a heart is never enjoyable. On the other hand, a path with heart is easy—it does not make a warrior work at liking it; it makes for a joyful journey; as long as a man follows it, he is one with it (Castaneda 1998, 19).

Regarding making decisions in our lives as to what paths to follow and what paths to avoid, the above words of Carlos Castaneda ring true and cannot be refuted. Use your heart as a GPS to guide you in the direction of your dreams. You will know when you are achieving the results you are striving for when your heart leaps for joy. A path with heart is formed by deliberately selecting a number of things that you want to involve yourself with: relationships, vocations, hobbies, arts, anything that connects your heart with the world. The criteria for selection are peace, joy, and strength.

Always Do Your Best

"I do the very best I know how, the very best I can, and I mean to keep doing so until the end."

—Abraham Lincoln

Doing your best in everything you do is a habit you can groom—the more you practice, the better you get. By consistently doing your best, your life improves dramatically, your self-respect increases, and so does your productivity. Doing your best is about taking action and doing what you love to do because your life will consist of actions that make you happy.

Always do your best. For sure, you can always do your best. And your best changes all the time—when you are sick or tired, your best is different than when you are awake and fresh. But by always doing your best, you are going to be content with yourself. If you make the choice to do your best and believe it, that is your best. You have the power to make the choice. And magic begins to happen in your life. This is the mastery of life. This is the path to personal freedom.

Under any circumstance simply do your best and you will avoid self-judgment, self-abuse and regret. Everything you have ever learned you have learned by repetition. You learned to write, to drive, and even to walk by repetition. Practice makes the master. By doing your best you become the master. If you do your best always, over and over again, you will become a master of transformation (Ruiz 1997, 76).

I know when I have done my best. I feel accomplished in new ways. I am able to unclutter my mind and redirect my energy into the next logical step or task that I should take, as well as set goals and actively reach them.

Do your best every day and be proud of yourself for your efforts. When you haven't done your best, forgive yourself, quickly move on, and commit to trying harder next time. Make doing your best a daily challenge in your life. If you approach a task, even something as minute as tying your shoes, with the mind-set that you are going to do it right the first time, it will keep you from spending the time redoing it. As the saying goes,

Time is money. If you do your best over and over again, you will enrich your life, become more productive, and improve your self-esteem.

Self-Importance Is Your Greatest Enemy

Self-importance is the belief that you are more important than everyone else. Exaggerating one's importance is often accompanied by arrogance, conceit, and egotistical behavior. Think about it. Our self-importance causes us to be offended by other people, what they say, and what they do. This is a huge waste of energy and our precious time. It weakens us.

Self-importance causes us to:

- Feel offended

- Defend our image

- Complain

- Reject ourselves

- Suffer needlessly

- Feel sorry for ourselves through exaggerated self-pity

- Think negatively

- Make everyone else wrong or become critical of others

- Defend our opinions

- Gossip about ourselves and others

How much time do we spend complaining about our problems, feeling offended about something someone said or did, or feeling sad and playing "Poor Me" through victimization? It is easy to play the guilt card, especially while experiencing symptoms from mental illness! But it is not worth it.

For example, you spend all day thinking about a girlfriend or boyfriend who pissed you off, whether you should stay with them, and wondering if you are wasting your time with this person. That night, you get into a car accident, and the last thought you have before you die is, "Man, I wasted the whole day feeling lousy when I should have been having fun, enjoying myself, and being thankful for just being alive".

Don't take yourself so seriously. Reducing self-importance frees up energy that can be rechanneled into furthering your goals, reduces negative thought patterns, eliminates needless anger and suffering, and increases happiness.

To free mental and emotional energy, annihilate the self-important patterns of behavior such as the presentation and defense of the self in everyday life, excessive routines, the tremendous insistence on the concerns of the self, and the incessant preoccupation with romantic courtship.

Stop the Internal Dialogue

The internal dialogue is the incessant voice in our heads that has been programmed and groomed to focus on our egos ever since we started to think. Our minds constantly focus on our internal dialogue (self-talk). Our self-talk programs and shapes our self-concept. For example, if you believe you are worthy and strong, you will live up to that truth. On the other hand, if you criticize yourself and tell yourself you will never get what you want, you won't. Conditioning yourself to stay in a positive mind frame does wonders for your overall mental health.

Autosuggestion

In his best-selling book *Think and Grow Rich*, Napoleon Hill explains a process called autosuggestion, which relies on the principle, "What you focus on, you attract."

> *Autosuggestion is the process of voluntarily fixing your attention upon a definite major purpose of a positive nature and forcing your mind through daily habits of thought, to dwell on that subject (Hill 1983, p.143).*

The dominating thoughts that you hold in your conscious mind act to magnetize your subconscious, and these "magnets" attract the forces, people, and circumstances of life that you desire. This is why visualizations and affirmations can have such a powerful effect in your life.

The language of the subconscious mind is feelings and emotions. Emotions are either positive or negative; both cannot occupy the mind at the same time. By focusing on positive emotions and banishing negative ones, you save up energy to expend on your definite major purpose instead of wasting your energy on negativity.

There are seven positive emotions and seven negative emotions that your subconscious understands:

Positive Emotions:

- Desire
- Faith
- Love
- Sex
- Enthusiasm
- Romance
- Hope

Negative Emotions

- Fear
- Jealousy
- Hatred
- Greed
- Vengefulness
- Superstition
- Anger

The process of autosuggestion consists of the following steps:

1. Decide on a major purpose you really want to accomplish.

2. Say this intention out loud every day: "My subconscious mind is my partner in success."

3. Concentrate on your major purpose and visualize what it will look and feel like when it comes true.

4. Flood your mind with positive emotions.

5. Stay alert and receptive of the ideas, people, and circumstances that show up in your life to aid you in the achievement of your major purpose.

6. Take action.

7. Spend ten minutes every day for a month following the above steps.

It is important to remember that taking steps to set your intentions is only effective if you make a consistent effort and you work toward putting your words into actions.

Death Is Stalking You

"Time waits for no man."

—Abraham Lincoln

A warrior uses death as their most important advisor. Warriors routinely ask the following questions:

1. If all I have is this moment, how do I want to use it?

2. Is this the best I can do?

3. Is this activity worthy of my life?

4. If I died right now, would my death respect me?

In a world where death is the hunter, there is no time for regrets or doubts. There is only time for decisions. Our most costly mistake as average men is indulging in a sense of immortality. It is as though we believe that if we don't think about death we can protect ourselves from it. Only the idea of death makes a warrior sufficiently detached so that he is capable of abandoning himself to anything. He knows his death is stalking him and won't give him time to cling to anything so he tries without craving all of everything (Teachings n. d.).

Using death as an advisor helps you to focus on what matters most and also makes things clear. Other concerns pale in comparison. Meaning wells up from your heart and you gain clarity on how you want to spend your time and live your life.

The following words from the movie *"Walk the Line"*, about the life of Johnny Cash, highlights the importance of using death as an advisor:

All right, let's bring it home. If you was hit by a truck, and you were lying out in that gutter dying, and you had time to sing one song, one song people would remember before you're dirt, one song that would let God know what you felt about your time here on earth, one song that would sum you up, are you telling me that's the song you'd sing, that same Jimmy Davis tune we hear on the radio all day, about your peace within and how it's real and how you're gonna shout it? Or, would you sing something different, something real, something you felt? 'Cause I'm telling you right now that's the kind of song people want to hear. That's the kind of song that truly saves people. It ain't got nothing to do with believing in God, Mr. Cash. It has to do with believing in yourself.

As I write this section in a Starbucks, a spry-looking lady of about sixty barely escaped slipping on the wet concrete outside, having a nasty fall, and perhaps splitting her skull. Luckily, she caught herself. Death is always a stone's throw away. Our time on earth is limited, and there is no time to be mediocre. Embrace your own essence and grab life by the horns!

Stalk Yourself

The "Art of Stalking" is a set of procedures and attitudes that enables you to get the best of any conceivable situation. For this discussion, stalking results in positive results and is not associated with doing any kind of harm to other people.

A friend of mine told me about a conversation he had with his son about the art of stalking:

My twenty-year-old son and I were sitting in a booth at Denny's waiting for his girlfriend to show up. He was getting irate because she was late. We reminisced, as we always did when the subject of being late came up, about his mom (my ex), who was habitually late and drove me and the kids crazy. He kept looking at his watch, and I knew he was going to jump his girlfriend's case when she arrived.

He calmed down when I asked him when he had to leave and go to work. He said he had an hour so there was no big hurry. I asked him if he had ever heard about stalking someone, not in the sense of intending to do them harm or being a predator, but in terms of gaining energy and not wasting it. He said, "No, what do you mean?" I explained that the art of stalking is a set of procedures and attitudes that would enable him to get the best of any situation.

I told him an example of stalking would be not to act irritated at his girlfriend when she arrived—don't show any negative emotion at all, but convince her it doesn't bother you one bit that she is late. If she says she is sorry for being late, simply say, "No problem, I don't have to leave for work for a while". I explained to him that acting in this manner, even if he was irritated on the inside, would keep him from wasting his energy being negative, she wouldn't feel bad, and we would have a much better time eating breakfast together. By following this course of action he would have successfully stalked her because she would treat him better and be more understanding when he did something that pissed her off.

Then I drove home the most important benefit of stalking. I told him that by stalking his girlfriend, he was actually stalking himself. By using his mind in a disciplined manner and choosing not to take her arriving late personally, he wouldn't cause himself or anyone else at the table needless suffering and save himself from expending energy unnecessarily.

Strange to stalk yourself, isn't it? Try it and see how effective it can be.

Because your mind is especially subject to the dominating influences in your environment, you must take control over those influences by developing beneficial mental habits. The process of controlling your habits is miraculous. It translates the power of thought into action. But if your habits are poor or bad, they can bring misery and failure. Your success depends on the strength and quality of your controlled habits (Hill 1983, 133).

Stop Defending Your Self-Image

Over the years you have built an idealized self-image that you defend as your sense of self. In this image are packed all the things you want to see as true about yourself; banished from it are all the shameful, guilty, and fear-provoking aspects that threaten your self-confidence. People spend a lot of time in therapy trying to turn a bad self-image into an acceptable one. As reasonable as that sounds, all self-images have the same pitfall: they keep reminding you of who you were, not who you are. The whole idea of I, me, and mine has been erected on memories, and these memories are not really you. Focus on the present and your sense of you will be the updated, positive one you want and desire.

Stop Trying to Make Others Wrong

To conserve energy, stop trying to make yourself right and others wrong. Everyone is a product of their environment and has formed an opinion about almost everything. If you stop caring whether you are right or wrong, then you will stop judging yourself and others and trying to prove that your opinion is superior to theirs. Most importantly, you will stop wasting your energy.

Accept Yourself

We are our own worst enemies due to the habit we have of criticizing and judging ourselves. We criticize ourselves a hundred times a day without even realizing it. Think about it—how often do you give yourself a hard time over past events, things you said, or past actions? The more emotion that was invested in the event, the more we criticize ourselves for the same transgression over and over again. Reduce the amount of time you spend criticizing yourself, and your mind will be more at peace.

Erase Personal History

For most people, personal history must be constantly renewed by telling parents, relatives, friends, and coworkers everything that we do or that happens to us. As a result, they pin us down with their thoughts and expectations. Erasing personal history frees us from the encumbering thoughts of other people. We are not defined by our past—the future is what matters.

Start keeping personal things to yourself that you normally would share with someone else. Slowly over time, tell people less and less about what you do and who you are. In this manner, you can begin to erase your personal history. Camouflage your personal history to keep from being pinned down by other people's thoughts or expectations. You need not be pigeonholed because you are bipolar, for example.

The benefits of erasing your personal history include:

1. No one pins you down with their thoughts or expectations.

2. You can re-create yourself into whomever you want to be.

3. Forgetting the past allows you to focus on what is happening now and stop wasting your energy mulling over past events.

Explanations are a sign of weakness. With every explanation, there is a hidden apology. An average man believes that his explanations of life will enable him to survive, but explanations are a meaningless waste of time. Understanding is a matter of experience, not the result of explanations. By erasing personal history, no explanations are needed, and nobody is angry or disillusioned with our acts.

Face Fear Head On

"Courage is being scared to death but saddling up anyway."

—John Wayne

Anytime you come up on something and the only thing that keeps you from doing it is fear, your decision is automatically made. You therefore look your fear straight in the eye and proceed in that direction.

Too often we allow fear, worry, and doubts to dominate and define our lives. We allow them to steal our joy, our sleep, and our precious dreams.

> *Your emotional posture is a major influence regarding how others relate to you and how you experience the world. If you're afraid of doing something, you're likely to avoid it or be timid doing it. At the same time, if you don't acknowledge negative feelings, you allow them to fester and thus diminish physical, mental, and emotional health. Worry, for example, warps energy. Enmeshed in the furrows of worry, people constantly struggle with and tear apart stabilizing energies such as control, patience, and timing. Thus people become accessible and lose their balance and their wits (Feather 2006, 234).*

There are several steps you can take to face fear:

1. Get comfortable with fear.

2. Make your dominant thoughts positive.

3. Don't give attention, energy, or time to fear.

4. Don't dwell on scarcity.

5. Laugh at your fear.

6. Tell yourself that in one hundred years, whatever happens as a result of you facing your fear won't matter.

7. View life as a wild adventure.

8. Plan to be great.

A powerful technique that can help you face fear is to visualize a positive end result and consider steps you can take until you know exactly what you need to do to succeed. For example, many of us are afraid of public speaking. In order to face that fear, set your intentions by planning your speech in your mind and then writing it down. Next, practice, practice, and practice in front of a mirror while visualizing the speech going smoothly and on course as planned. When you first walk up in front of your audience, pause and take three breaths before you begin to speak. When you begin to talk say something funny. The audience will relax, and so will you. Finally, instead of standing still and not moving while delivering your speech, recite a paragraph and then move to the left or to the right a few steps and continue.

I used the above advice when I spoke at my Dad's funeral. Writing the speech down was the key, as well as practicing in front of a mirror. The end result was that I was able to honor his life and felt grateful for being able to do so.

Running the Bipolar Marathon

Battling bipolar disorder is a lifelong war that can be compared to running a marathon. Marathon runners train, train, train, and then run the race to the best of their ability. Keep these steps in mind for running your personal bipolar marathon:

1. There are good days and bad days, and sometimes you can't tell the difference until you start.

2. Contrary to popular belief, sleep is not overrated—not in the slightest.

3. Don't forget to breathe.

4. Just because it's raining doesn't mean you should cry.

5. Nobody ever said it was easy.

6. Pain is temporary, but pride lasts a lifetime.

7. Create a plan and stick to it. It may not always work, but if you stay focused and relaxed, it will end up just fine.

8. You've got to try no matter what happens. In the end, you'll have bigger regrets from not trying at all.

9. Strength and courage blossom from the seeds of adversity.

10. Sometimes it's the little things that make the biggest differences.

11. Making it to the starting line is usually a lot harder than getting to the finish.

12. Listen to your body and listen to your mind. Make sure you acknowledge when they may be lying to you.

13. You can't change the past, and you won't alter the future. Enjoy your life in the present and always be positive!

14. Smile—it is contagious and increases endorphins. It actually takes more muscles and energy to frown.

15. It is okay to cry.

16. Don't forget to eat. Food can dictate your mood. If you take medication in the morning like I do, it is critical to eat to stabilize your sugar level and brain chemicals.

"*God gave me a great body, and it's my duty to take care of my physical temple.*"
—Jean-Claude Van Damme, Actor
Diagnosed with Bipolar Disorder

CHAPTER **9**

Train Your Body

If you take care of your body, your body will in turn take care of you. Your mind and body are a unit; being good to your body benefits your mind. Taking care of your body will help stabilize your mood and maximize your energy for the battles ahead.

What you do to exercise your body is important, but what you don't do to your body is more important. By avoiding anything that is harmful, you will not obstruct the way your body naturally functions, and in return, your body will take care of you.

Consistent application of several or all of the following actions will tune your body and improve your physical health.

It is Crucial to Get Enough Sleep

For those of us who are bipolar it is **CRUCIAL** to get enough sleep. Lack of sleep is one of the strongest triggers of a bipolar episode (Kvarnstorm, 2018). If you are having trouble sleeping, get a sleep aid from your psychiatrist. You can also try taking Melatonin or ZzzQuil if you want to try something over the counter. Meditation and herbal tea may also help.

Stay Away from Sick People at All Costs

I have an extreme phobia of being around people who are sick. If someone around you is sick (coughing, fever, etc.), or tells you they have recently been sick, immediately distance yourself from them, even if you have to make a scene, like moving to a new seat in a movie theater. Just move away. I follow this rule whether I'm in line at the grocery, at the office, visiting my family, or anywhere else. Sometimes sick people will physically infringe on me, like coming into my cubicle at work to talk, attending a meeting I am at, or standing in close proximity to me. At times it seems like this person who is sick wants to get close to me so they can give the illness away. Don't let them infect you, life is way too short to be sick, especially if you could have done something about it. Living with bipolar disorder is hard enough.

May 1, 2020: I wrote the paragraph above in December 2019, before the advent of the Corona Virus (COVID 19) pandemic currently spreading across the globe. Now it is more important than ever to heed this advice. In fact, it could be a matter of life or death. As of today there have been 3,300,000 confirmed cases of COVID 19 worldwide, resulting in 235,000 deaths and 1,040,000 recoveries from the epidemic. The United States is the country which has been hit the hardest by COVID 19, with 1,130,000 confirmed cases resulting in 65,253 deaths and 137,000 recoveries. Scientists are scrambling to find a vaccine as the virus continues to wreak havoc around the world.

One technique that I have used over the past 3 years is to frequently blow my nose throughout the day and keep my nasal passages clear. I haven't been sick since I implemented this method.

Also, to ward off disease and to feel better about yourself, brush your teeth regularly and use mouthwash.

Stay Hydrated

Pay attention to what your body is telling you—when you feel thirsty, replenish. It is important to flush your system and hydrate. In addition, fluids are very helpful when you are trying to lose weight because it reduces your appetite. Staying hydrated also helps your mind function more effectively.

Eat Healthy

Eat protein (steak, chicken, eggs, cheese), as well as salads, veggies, and fruit. Cut back on the bad carbohydrates (white bread, pasta, sweets). Good carbohydrates include rice, fruit, and potatoes. As with all things, balance is the key.

Make Love

Having sex with someone I like and who likes me back always energizes me and makes me feel better. I don't believe I am alone in these feelings. Intimacy as well as pleasure is good for us due to the dopamine released during sex. It is a natural "high" that is your body's way of saying, "Thanks. I needed that!"

In his book, *Think and Grow Rich*, Napoleon Hill talks about the benefits of sex for maintaining good health:

> *Sex desire is the most powerful of human emotions. For this very reason, the emotion of sex as a therapeutic agency for maintaining good health has no equal.*

The emotions are states of mind. When the emotion of love begins to mix itself with the emotion of sex, the result is calmness of purpose, poise, accuracy of judgement and balance. When love, romance, and sex are combined, these three emotions can lift one to the status of a genius (Hill 1983, p. 160).

Get Fresh Air and Sunshine

Getting fresh air every day clears your head, calms you down, and helps you appreciate the fact that you are alive on this awesome earth. Soak up the sun when you can. Looking directly at the sun with your eyes squinted just for a second or two is a way of gathering energy.

Stretch Your Body Every Day

Stretch your arms, legs, torso, and neck every day. Try to stay supple. This is especially important after sitting for extended periods of time.

Exercise

If you take care of your body, it will take care of you. Take walks, run, ride your bike, lift weights, dance, use the elliptical, do yoga, play basketball—do anything you enjoy that gets the blood pumping.

We are all different physically, and our energy levels vary from person to person. Start at whatever level you are now, and slowly increase your prowess. Build a strong core. In anatomy, the core refers to the body except for the legs and arms. The core is the power center. Besides the physical benefits, a strong core increases your willpower and sharpens your gut instincts.

The core is one of the most important parts of the body to exercise and strengthen. Functional movements are highly dependent on the core, and lack of core development can result in a predisposition to injury. The major muscles of the core reside in the area of the belly, the middle and lower back, and peripherally the hips, the shoulders, and the neck.

You may find it easier to accomplish these actions if you incorporate them into your schedule on a consistent basis—for example, take walks every other day during your lunch break.

Drugs and Alcohol

More than 40 percent of us who are bipolar abuse alcohol or drugs, sometimes in an attempt to self-medicate (Cerullo, 2007). If you drink or do drugs, evaluate whether they are keeping you from being your best self. Also be mindful to consider whether you may be overdoing it to mask or numb your emotions. Drugs and alcohol can trigger an episode if you aren't careful, so treat them with respect.

I'm not preaching here. Believe me, I can relate. I used to smoke pot every day if I had a supply. My favorite brand was White Widow. When I was smoking, it was all or nothing. I used to tell myself I was a better man when I was stoned, with more energy and creativity, like Popeye eating spinach. However, after being in a couple of car wrecks because I was stoned out of my mind, and realizing that weed was a contributing factor in my bipolar episodes, I admitted to myself that pot was more detrimental than beneficial for me. It wasn't easy to quit—marijuana is a powerful force. For several months after I quit smoking, I had dreams in which I was rolling joints from a large bag of Sensimilla containing huge, beautiful, moist, aromatic buds and then toking it up. Now that I have quit, I don't have the urge to smoke anymore. I can be around people who are smoking and I am not tempted. But to be clear, I am highly cognizant that if I

BREAKING BIPOLAR • 120

get high even once I will be back to smoking every day, probably like people in AA know if they take one drink, they are going to get drunk, and getting back on the wagon is going to be a bitch.

As I said, I have finally been able to stop smoking pot altogether. However, I still drink alcohol a couple of times a week. For now, this is the approach that is working for me. You will need to figure out what works best for you.

I like this passage found in the book *The Outsider* by Stephen King, which emphasizes the ritual casting off of bad habits and improving one's mental health:

> *Holly paused, looking down at her hands. The nails were unpolished, but quite neat; she had quit chewing them, just as she had quit smoking. Broken herself of the habit. She sometimes thought that her pilgrimage to something at least approximating mental stability (if not genuine mental health) had been marked by the ritual casting off of bad habits. It had been hard to let them go. They were friends (King 2018, p. 415).*

As an alternative to self-medicating with drugs and alcohol, learn to use bipolar medications to your advantage instead. Bipolar medications are very powerful pharmaceutical drugs and if used intelligently can work wonders.

Shed Extra Pounds

Losing weight is one of the hardest things to do. However, it is worth it. Your body functions better and your energy levels are higher when you aren't carrying too many extra pounds. As mentioned in the "Bipolar Disorder Facts and Statistics" section in Chapter 5, approximately 25 percent of people with bipolar disorder are overweight, and sometimes obese. The good news is that being overweight can be controlled. By changing your diet, you can effectively lose weight and keep the pounds off.

My weight has fluctuated over the years. I will go on sprees in which I binge on barbecue chips, sweets, ice cream, and Margaritas. Needless to say, I put on extra pounds during these times of lower will power, especially in the winter time around the holidays. All of a sudden, I have gained 10 to 15 pounds and tend to start giving myself a hard time many times a day until I gather enough willpower to begin dieting.

I have been very successful losing weight with the diet described below, when I am disciplined enough to stick with it. This diet is a modified version of the Atkins diet. I have used this diet two times in the last 10 years and lost at least 12 pounds each time. I am convinced it will work for anyone. Run it by your doctor if you would like to get their input, but feel at ease knowing the food allowed on the diet is healthy.

Try following this diet for two months to lose weight:

1. Stop eating sweets.

2. Limit the amount of carbs you eat, especially in the first three to four weeks. This is key.

3. Drink a lot of fluids, especially water. It is not necessary to stop drinking coffee if you are so inclined.

4. Eat protein: steak, chicken, pork, cheese, eggs, etc.

5. Eat salads with veggies like radishes, carrots, broccoli, and cauliflower.

6. Eat fruits like melon, blackberries, avocados, and grapes.

7. Eat small amounts of nuts such as macadamia nuts, almonds and cashews.

8. If you drink alcohol, drink Michelob Ultra for beer, or shots without mixers.

9. During the first two weeks on the diet, minimize your calorie intake without starving yourself. Your belly will start to shrink so you aren't as hungry. At some point, you will feel your metabolism speeding up and your body will go into fat-burning mode.

10. Follow an exercise schedule doing what you like to do best.

11. Be patient and give it time.

When you begin losing weight, your motivation and sense of accomplishment will grow, and make it easier to stick with the diet.

Maintaining your weight is a lifestyle change. Once you reach your target weight, be mindful that gaining weight is much easier and takes a lot less time than losing weight. If you stop watching what you eat, you will gain the weight back, and the sacrifice, and extraordinary willpower you spent dieting will be for naught.

Get Your Thyroid Checked

Much of our day-to-day well-being—how energetic we feel, how clear our thinking is and how our body processes food is governed by the activity of the butterfly-shaped, thumb-sized thyroid gland at the base of the throat. When it is working as it should, life is good. However, keep in mind that more than 12 percent of the U.S. population will develop a thyroid condition during their lifetime (American Thyroid Association, 2020). The good news is that thyroid disease can be managed with medication.

Hypothyroidism (underactive thyroid) occurs when the thyroid gland does not produce enough hormones. If your thyroid hormone levels are too low, you may have fatigue, digestive problems, sensitivity to cold temperatures, and menstrual irregularities. If left untreated hypothyroidism can lead to many complications. These include heart problems, nerve injury, infertility and in severe cases, death (Madhusoodanan, 2019).

Hyperthyroidism (overactive thyroid) occurs when your thyroid gland produces too much of the hormone thyroxine. Hyperthyroidism can accelerate your body's metabolism, causing unintentional weight loss and a rapid or irregular heartbeat (Mayo Clinic, 2020).

Thyroid disease is associated with bipolar disorder and can actually cause bipolar symptoms as well as diabetes. Anyone who is bipolar should get your thyroid checked. There is a simple blood test that measures the amount of Thyroid Stimulating Hormone (TSH) in the body. Thyroid medicine can correct either a hypothyroid or hyperthyroid condition, both of which can mimic the symptoms of bipolar disorder (Chakrabarti, 2011), (Bocchetta, 2016), (Hage, 2011).

Back in 2001, eight years after my first bipolar episode, my psychiatrist ordered a thyroid test as part of my regularly scheduled blood test to check my Lithium level. The results of the test showed that I have a hypothyroid condition, and I have been taking Levothyroxine on a daily basis ever since. I weighed 210 pounds at the time, and after being on thyroid medication for about four months, I was able to lose 30 pounds and have pretty much maintained the same weight ever since. I attribute the weight loss to having a faster metabolism brought about by treating my hypothyroidism condition.

Note: Taking Lithium every day for a long time can cause thyroid problems as well as impact kidney function (Surks, 2019). If you take Lithium then your doctor will have you take blood tests for Lithium levels and kidney functioning on a quarterly basis.

There are measures you can take to treat a thyroid condition, other than taking medication. Three of these include:

1. Keep up your mineral levels. The thyroid needs iodine to churn out hormones, and usually iodized salt or sea salt with natural iodine can supply most of our daily need of 150 micrograms.

2. Filter drinking water. Fluoride and chlorine are elements that can block the absorption of iodine into the thyroid.

3. Talk it out. In Eastern philosophy, the thyroid is located at the fifth chakra, the energy center of expression and communication. If you find yourself either regularly shouting or choking back your words, to support your thyroid on a deep emotional level, express yourself regularly to someone such as a therapist, family member or good friend (Natural Endocrine Solutions, 2018).

Make an appointment with an endocrinologist and get your thyroid checked out.

Take Vitamins

There are definite benefits in taking vitamins:

Vitamin B helps prevent infections and helps support cell health, growth of red blood cells, energy levels, good eyesight, healthy brain function, good digestion, healthy appetite, and proper nerve function (Cronkleton, 2019).

Vitamin C, also known as ascorbic acid, is necessary for the growth, development and repair of all body tissues. It's involved in many body functions, including formation of collagen, absorption of iron, the immune system, wound healing, and the maintenance of cartilage, bones, and teeth (Zelman, 2010).

Vitamin D is necessary for building and maintaining healthy bones, because calcium, the primary component of bone, can only be absorbed by your body when vitamin D is present. Your body makes vitamin D when direct sunlight converts a chemical in your skin into an active form of the vitamin (calciferol) (Mayo Clinic, 2017).

Benefits of Natural Herbs and Spices

Fish Oil (Omega-3 Fatty Acids): Your brain is made up of nearly 60% fat, and much of this fat is omega-3 fatty acids. Therefore, omega-3s are essential for normal brain function. Research suggests that fish oil supplements can prevent the onset or improve the symptoms of some mental disorders. For example, it can reduce the chances of psychotic disorders in those who are at risk. Food sources of omega-3 fatty acids include salmon, albacore tuna, flaxseed and walnuts (Robertson, 2018).

Garlic: Garlic is low in calories and rich in vitamin C, vitamin B6 and manganese. It also contains trace amounts of various other nutrients. Garlic can combat sickness, including flu and the common cold. Garlic can reduce blood pressure, improve cholesterol levels which may lower the risk of heart disease, contains antioxidants that may help prevent Alzheimer's disease and dementia, may help you live longer, may help detoxify heavy metals in the body and may improve bone health (Leech, 2018).

Bulk up on garlic when you start to feel sick. One tasty way to eat garlic is to cut up fresh garlic and cook it in the oven or on the stovetop with olive oil until slightly crispy.

Cinnamon: Cinnamon is loaded with antioxidants, has anti-inflammatory properties, may cut the risk of heart disease, can improve sensitivity to the hormone insulin, lowers blood sugar levels and has a powerful anti-diabetic effect, may have beneficial effects on neurodegenerative diseases, may protect against cancer, helps fight bacterial and fungal infections and may help fight the HIV virus (Leech, 2018).

Curry: This spice boosts your immune system, can relieve the pain of arthritis, may help to prevent Alzheimer's and cancer, is good for your heart, can help ease digestion, helps lower your cholesterol and boosts your metabolism (Mann, 2016).

Cardamom: This spice may lower blood pressure, may contain cancer-fighting compounds, may protect from chronic diseases, may help with digestive problems, including ulcers, may treat bad breath and prevent cavities, may have antibacterial effects and treat infections, may improve breathing and oxygen use and may lower blood sugar levels (Streit, 2018).

Cloves: Cloves contain fiber, vitamins, and minerals, are high in antioxidants, may help protect against cancer, can kill bacteria, may improve liver health, may help regulate blood sugar, may promote bone health and may reduce stomach ulcers (Link, 2020).

Take Showers or Baths

It is surprising how good it feels to take a shower or bath. Cleansing yourself with water relaxes you and makes you feel clean and refreshed. Take a long shower or bath to spend time focusing on yourself. Add candles, therapeutic salts, or your favorite music as enhancements. Just splashing cold water on your face is reviving.

Animal Lovers

Caring for an animal can provide companionship and be therapeutic and rewarding. It is nice to have a feeling of being loved every time you come home. Unconditional love from a pal who needs you and always cares can be a key to maintaining consistent mental health. Another benefit is that you get more exercise, fresh air and sunshine when you take your dog on walks. It has been proven that petting a cat or dog can improve and enhance our mood (Healthessentials, 2020).

"I spent a year in a 12-step program, really committed, because I could not believe what had happened—that I might have killed myself."

—Carrie Fisher, Actress, Screenwriter
Diagnosed with Bipolar Disorder

CHAPTER **10**

Recovering from a
Bipolar Episode

No matter how down or out of control you feel, it's important to remember that you are not powerless when it comes to recovering from a bipolar episode. This chapter offers a number of tactics and strategies that can speed up your recovery.

For each of my three bipolar episodes, I began the recovery process while I was in a psychiatric hospital, and then continued recovering after I was discharged from the hospital; the first time at home (when I was married with four kids), the second time when I was living by myself, and after my third bipolar episode I recovered at my daughters house. Recovering from my first and third bipolar episodes was extremely difficult and it took about two months until I felt like I had things under control again and was back on an even keel. Surprisingly, I recovered fairly quickly after my second bipolar episode (see Chapter 1, The Hospital Roof), and only missed 6 days of work, perhaps because I was off my medications for a much shorter time (5 days), and after being manic I didn't sink into depression.

Some of the things that helped me recover from my episodes include:

Work Closely with your Psychiatrist Regarding Medications

Medication is a big factor that impacts the length of time it takes to recover from a bipolar episode. If the episode was severe, then you may have been heavily medicated with high dosages of strong pharmaceutical medications to bring your symptoms into check. Once your mood stabilizes and your symptoms subside, your psychiatrist will most likely make changes to the medications and/or dosages you are taking. Work closely with your psychiatrist to find the medication cocktail that works best for you.

Have Your Own Space

One thing that was crucial after coming home from the hospital was to have a place I could retreat to and be by myself. This was especially important in the beginning because my mood was still cycling and I felt very shaky, anxious, and at times almost out of control. It took me a couple of weeks until I wanted to be around people more than a short amount of time.

Understand Recovery Takes Time

Recovery does not happen overnight. You should not expect an immediate 100 percent recovery after an episode. As with any illness, there is a period of convalescence. Stability initially means taking things slowly. True healing is not just about getting rid of mood swings; it's about letting your brain and body get back on track.

It often feels like a bipolar episode results in lost time—time lost doing what you would normally do or living how you normally would. After an episode, I look at the wreckage left behind and feel overwhelmed with the task of rebuilding. It is normal to wish we could feel better in a quicker manner or to worry that we may never feel the same. But working too hard at it can result in burnout and lack of rest can even trigger another episode.

John talks about returning home from a psychiatric hospital after experiencing a bipolar episode:

> I had a manic episode that resulted in me being involuntarily committed to a psychiatric hospital. They dosed me with some powerful medicines and four days later, after I stabilized, I convinced the psychiatrist who was treating me to discharge me from the hospital. When I got home, I had to deal with side effects from the medications. My hands were trembling so much I couldn't sign my name on checks and withdrawal slips. I was taking a class for college and could only concentrate for a short amount of time. Not to mention returning to work. It took me about a month to start feeling myself again.

Contacting Your Employer

If you are going to miss work because of a bipolar episode, it's important to contact your boss and/or Human Resources as soon as you feel up to it and let them know you won't be coming to work for a few days and will be back as soon as you can. Before you make the call, decide how much you want to divulge. You don't necessarily have to say you are recovering from a bipolar episode, but saying you haven't been feeling well and are under a doctor's care can be a valid excuse for missing work. If you are in the hospital, once you feel ready, tell the charge nurse you need to call your boss and they will facilitate the call. Eventually you may have to own up as to why you missed work but you can cross that bridge down the road. Once you make the phone call, a huge weight will fall off your shoulders and allow you to focus your energies on your recovery.

Monitor your Moods and Symptoms

While recovering from a bipolar episode it is important to recognize the lingering symptoms you are having due to the illness, as well as the warning signs of a relapse into a manic or depressive episode. If you are having troublesome symptoms or your mood is fluctuating toward mania or depression, make an appointment to see your psychiatrist as soon as you can.

Eliminate Stress

Know your limits, both at home, at work, or at school. Don't take on more than you can handle, and make it a priority to make time for you if you are feeling overwhelmed. When you are recovering from an episode, some of the same things that were stressing you out and were instrumental in triggering your episode may still be present. These stressors could be a spouse, roommate, your kids, bills, a sick relative or other factors.

Bipolar Support Groups

The last thing I wanted to do after being released from the hospital was attend a support group. But after a few weeks of attending support group meetings I realized that no matter how I felt before the meetings and no matter what was discussed during them, I always left feeling better.

Just being around people who were engaged in similar struggles—even if they didn't have all the answers, even if they did their fair share of complaining, even if I disagreed with some of what they said- helped.

The wonder of working with a collective is that you get to learn from everyone within it. Often the best lessons came from those who are struggling the most. Because I had the chance to learn lessons vicariously through members of my support group, I have been able to avoid a great deal of suffering and heartache.

My takeaway from the most recent bipolar support group meeting I attended, was when one of the members said, "I never know if I am doing bipolar correctly." This resonated powerfully with me.

There are support groups for bipolars only, as well as support groups for both the bipolar individual and a support person such as their significant other or friend.

Do an online search to find a bipolar support group in your area or an online support group. Here are a couple of websites that could be helpful:

Depression Bipolar Support Alliance:
https://www.dbsalliance.org/support/

The 7 Best Online Bipolar Disorder Support Groups of 2020:
https://www.verywellmind.com/best-online-bipolar-disorder-support-groups-4802211

Use Coping Techniques

There are many things you can do to reduce your symptoms and stay on track, including educating yourself about bipolar disorder, surrounding yourself with people you can count on, and leading a healthy "wellness" lifestyle. With good coping skills and a solid support system, you can keep the symptoms of bipolar disorder in check, maintain your balance, and live fully and productively.

Here is a list of coping techniques that can help you recover from a bipolar episode:

- Talk to a supportive person

- Get a full eight hours of sleep

- Cut back on your activities

- Attend a support group

- Meet with your psychiatrist or therapist

- Do something fun or creative, or write in your journal

- Take time for yourself to relax and unwind

- Increase your exposure to light

- Exercise

- Eat healthy foods

- Cut back on sugar

- Avoid alcohol and drugs

- Increase or decrease the stimulation in your environment

- Take adequate breaks of relaxation

- Take a nature walk

- Spend time with your loved ones

- Take a bath or a nap (Sheehan, 2008)

Accept You Have a Biological Illness and Forgive Yourself

It makes a big difference if you accept the fact that your bipolar illness is caused by a chemical imbalance in your brain (Bressert, 2020). When you accept you have an actual disease, you can begin to forgive yourself for the bad things that happened during your episode. There is no use in worrying over past events that can't be changed, so don't cry over spilt milk. Focus your energy fully on recovery.

Take Care of Business

Talking with creditors, teachers or professors at school, or people you may have hurt emotionally or physically is never easy, but I can say from personal experience that life can be even better than it was before if you face the rebuilding process head-on, no matter how much it might hurt.

Set Goals for Yourself

Identifying life goals is the essential heart of the recovery process. When we identify and envision a future for ourselves, we begin to become motivated to do all we can to reach those goals. Your goals can be big or small, depending on where you are in your recovery journey.

Remember to break your goals into small steps at first. Ask yourself what you can do now that will help you accomplish your goal. Not only will this help move you closer to your goal, but it will also give you a positive feeling of accomplishment.

When you are setting your goals ask yourself the following questions:

1. What motivates me?

2. What interests me?

3. What would I do more of if I could?

4. What do I want?

5. What do I care about, or what did I care about before my illness or episode?

6. Where do I want my life to go?

7. What brings me joy?

8. What are my hopes and dreams?

Reach out for Face-to-Face Connection

Having a strong support system is essential to staying happy and healthy. Often, simply having someone to talk to face-to-face can be an enormous help in your road to recovery following an episode, as well as boost your outlook and motivation. The people you turn to don't have to be able to "fix" you; they just need to be good listeners. The more people that you can turn to who are available, dependable, and act as good listeners, the better you can manage your moods.

Get Therapy

While medication may be able to help you manage the symptoms of bipolar disorder, therapy teaches you skills you can use in all areas of your life, and can be a powerful weapon on the road to full recovery. Therapy can help you learn how to deal with your illness, cope with problems, regulate your mood, change the way you think, and improve your relationships.

Therapy can teach you to:

- Understand your illness

- Overcome fears or insecurities

- Cope with stress

- Make sense of past traumatic experiences

- Separate your true personality from the mood swings caused by your illness

- Identify triggers that may worsen your symptoms

- Improve relationships with family and friends

- Establish a stable, dependable routine

- Develop a plan for coping with crisis

- Understand why things bother you and what you can do to alleviate these issues

- End destructive habits such as drinking, using drugs, overspending, or risky sex

- Address symptoms such as changes in eating or sleeping habits, anger, anxiety, irritability, or unpleasant feelings (Swartz, 2014), (WebMD, 2020)

Dealing with the People Closest to You

While the things that you do and the way you behave during a bipolar episode vary widely in severity, they are sometimes very disturbing, frightening, threatening, or intolerable. Sometimes sustaining a relationship with a significant other or family member is complicated due to financial insecurity, infidelity, alcoholism, addiction, abusiveness, criminal activity, or other factors that may be associated with the illness.

When your episode ends and you begin the recovery process, do your best to make any amends that need to be made with your significant other, family, friends, or roommate. If they seem supportive and want to help, it can be extremely beneficial to include them in your treatment plan. The people in your life want you to get better because they care for you. They also want to protect themselves. They can help you spot symptoms, track behaviors, and gain perspective. They can also give encouraging feedback and help you make a plan to cope with any future crises.

Make a pact with your significant other or people you spend the most time with that if you begin exhibiting manic or depressive symptoms, they should bring it to your attention. Make a point of also being receptive to hearing people out if they express noticeable changes in your moods or behaviors.

As you can imagine, sometimes you need to set limits with the people you spend time with when you are recovering from a bipolar episode. In most cases they are trying to help you in your recovery but sometimes the things they do or say are unhelpful. If being around someone is not beneficial to your recovery process you might want to put some distance between you and them. You can always renew your relationship once you are back in control of your faculties.

Ruth tells about when she came home from the psychiatric hospital after a bipolar episode:

> *It's enough of a pain when you start second guessing or fearing what your mood might do, but one of the things I*

struggle with is when the people around me symptom check. If I laugh too loud, I'm quizzed if I'm still taking my meds. People will make remarks if my speech is rapid or tell me I "seem restless" and accuse me of "getting high" if I'm a bit more animated than usual.

Things People Do That Do Not Aid in Your Recovery

- Conveying that they are holier than you, nagging, preaching, or lecturing

- Asking how you are doing too frequently

- Watching and observing you all the time

- Analyzing and picking apart every thought, feeling and action that you have

- Checking if you are having symptoms too often

- Trying to make you dependent on them

- Not allowing you to handle situations on your own

- Not respecting your independence

Make a Battle Plan to Keep From Having Future Episodes

"The definition of insanity is doing the same thing over and over again, but expecting different results."

—Albert Einstein

The best advice I can offer when you are recovering from a bi-polar episode is to make a plan to keep from having future epi-sodes and put the plan into action.

As mentioned previously, successful treatment of bipolar disor-der depends on diligently following a comprehensive treatment plan including medication, educating yourself about the illness, communicating with your psychiatrist and therapist, having a strong support system, and helping yourself by making healthy lifestyle choices (WebMD, 2020).

Once you are feeling better and thinking clearly, recall the events and circumstances leading up to your bipolar episode, and identify what you could have done differently to keep the episode from happening. Then follow the instructions in Chapter 3 of this book, or however you prefer, to create a battle plan that includes the lessons you learned from your episode, and the treatment strategies mentioned in the previous paragraph. To achieve the best results, put your plan in writing and take action to further your plan on a daily basis.

The good news is that bipolar disorder responds very well to the right medication, therapy, and self-help strategies and skills. Do your best, and then some, to put the episode behind you and fo-cus on your recovery.

Rise up from the ashes and emerge stronger than you were before!

"I know the voices aren't real, but man do they ever come up with some great ideas."
—Jack Nicholson, Actor
Played part of mental patient in movie
"One Flew Over The Cuckoo's Nest"

Chapter 11

What You Need to Know about Psychiatric Hospitals

Bipolar episodes can sometimes end with a stay in a psychiatric hospital, either by voluntarily checking yourself in or being involuntarily committed. Hopefully you will never need to go into the hospital. However, if you do, knowing what to expect is very helpful and can speed up the time it takes for you to recover.

It is an extremely hard decision to check yourself into a psychiatric hospital. However, when bipolar symptoms become severe and you are in the throes of a full-blown manic or depressive episode, checking yourself into the hospital can be the best possible move. Being in a psychiatric hospital is similar to being in any other hospital: you are there to heal, calm down, and be safe.

If you think you should check into a psychiatric hospital, do it before things go from bad to worse. Sometimes those of us with bipolar disorder need help and asking for it, although difficult, can help you avoid disaster. If you feel you do not have the strength to do it alone, find someone who supports you to take you to the hospital.

Get help so that you can live to fight another day. Dire consequences of not getting help can include suicide, self-mutilation, physical violence, or other catastrophic results. Recall that up to 20% of us end our lives by suicide, and 20-60% of us attempt suicide at least once in our lifetime (Dome, 2019).

Voluntary Check-In

Three ways to check yourself into a psychiatric hospital include:

1. Go directly to a psychiatric hospital and tell them you need to be admitted. They will then ask you questions, and based on your answers and the amount of available space, they will admit you or deny you. Most times, if you say you are suicidal at your evaluation, that's sufficient evidence for immediate admittance.

2. Work with your psychiatrist to be admitted.

3. Go to the emergency room of a hospital and tell them exactly what's going on and what you are thinking. They will transport you to a psychiatric hospital.

When you arrive at a psychiatric hospital, you will go to the Screening and Admissions Unit where you will be asked to sign a voluntary evaluation and admission form. Next, you will be examined by a hospital physician. If the physician agrees that you should be hospitalized, you will then be admitted.

Involuntary Commitment

Involuntary commitment is the act of placing someone into a psychiatric hospital or similar facility without their consent. Although such action may seem harsh, it is sometimes necessary in order to prevent people from harming themselves or others and to ensure that appropriate treatment is administered. Involuntary commitment is discussed in more detail in Chapter 12, Legal Rights.

Reasons to Check into a Psychiatric Hospital

- You are having thoughts of hurting yourself or others.

- You are having hallucinations.

- You feel unsafe, like you might lose control and start beating your head against the wall, jump off of a bridge or some other dangerous act.

- You are having bizarre or paranoid ideas (delusions).

- You have not ate or slept for several days.

- You have serious problems with alcohol or drugs.

- You are thinking or talking too fast, jumping from topic to topic, or not making sense.

- You feel too exhausted or too depressed to get out of bed or take care of yourself or your family.

- You have tried outpatient treatment (therapy, medication, and support) and still have symptoms that interfere with your life.

- You need to make a major change in your treatment or medication under the close supervision of your doctor.

I have been in a psychiatric hospital three times due to bipolar episodes. I voluntarily checked myself in when I had my first episode in 1993, and was involuntarily committed for my second major episode in 2005 and my third major episode in 2012. The following is a list of things I learned along the way that can speed up your recovery if you find yourself in a psychiatric hospital.

BREAKING BIPOLAR • 146

Go with the Flow

An important thing to keep in mind when recovering from a bipolar episode in a psychiatric hospital is to go with the flow, rather than trying to fight it. You should trust that the psychiatrist and the nursing staff who are treating you want you to get better and are trying to help. It is in your best interest to cooperate with them and take their advice. You will be in a structured environment where there are set rules to follow. You have set times to wake up and go to sleep, take medications, eat meals, attend group therapy, etc. The more you cooperate, the sooner you will begin to recover, and the sooner the psychiatrist will sign your discharge papers.

Contacting Your Employer from the Hospital

If you are in the hospital and you haven't let your boss know you will be missing work, when you feel up to it, tell the charge nurse you need to call your boss and they will facilitate the call. Decide how much you want to divulge—you don't necessarily have to say you are in a psychiatric hospital, but saying you haven't been feeling yourself and you are in the hospital trying to find out what's wrong can be a valid excuse for missing work. Eventually you may have to own up that you are or were in a psychiatric hospital, but you can cross that bridge down the road. Once you make the phone call a huge weight will fall off your shoulders and you can then fully focus on your recovery.

How Hospitalization Can Help

Hospitalization can help in the following ways:

- The hospital is a safe place where you can begin to get well. It is a place to get away from the stresses that may be worsening your mood disorder and symptoms.

- It's a private way to get help when you need it. You don't have to tell anyone from outside the hospital where you are, even your family, if you choose not to.

- You can work with professionals to stabilize your severe symptoms, keep yourself safe, and learn new ways to cope with your illness.

- You can talk about traumatic experiences and explore your thoughts, ideas, and feelings openly.

- You can learn more about events, people, or situations that may trigger your manic or depressive episodes and how to cope with or avoid them.

- You may find a new treatment or combination of treatments that work.

- You will have time to reflect on your current situation and what improvements you can make.

The Ins and Outs of Psychiatric Hospitals

Things to know if you are in a psychiatric hospital include:

- Whether you are a voluntary check-in or involuntary commitment it is up to the psychiatrist treating you to decide when you can be discharged from the hospital. They must grant you permission to leave—you can't just check out.

- You can make a reasonable number of phone calls.

- You have the legal right to decide who can visit you and must sign a form giving them the right to do so.

- Your medicine will be dispensed to you at set times and a staff member will verify that you take the medicine.

- You will have to follow a schedule. There will be set times for meals, treatments, medications, activities, and bedtime.

- You may have physical or mental health tests. You may have blood tests to determine your medication levels or look for other physical problems that may be worsening your illness.

- You might have to ask for things you need more than once.

- Make sure that the doctor and the staff know about any other illnesses you have or medications you take. Be sure that you are receiving these medications.

- Your prescribing doctor may not be able to see you right away. You will probably talk to several different doctors, nurses, and staff members.

- You will meet other people who are working to overcome their own problems and interact with them. Treat them with courtesy and respect, regardless of what they may say or do. If someone is making you feel uncomfortable or unsafe, tell a staff member.

- Some of the people you meet may be able to relate to you and understand what you are going through. It may be a way for you to build or strengthen your support group.

- You may be in a locked ward. At first you may not be able to leave the ward. Later, you may be able to go to other parts of the hospital or get a pass to leave the hospital for a short time.

- You may have jewelry, personal care items, belts, shoelaces, or other personal belongings locked away during your stay. You may not be allowed to have items with glass or sharp edges, such as picture frames, CD cases, or spiral notebooks.

- You may share a room with someone else.

- In many places, the staff will not allow you to stay in your room for extended periods of time during the day. If you stay in your room, they may assume you are isolating yourself and keep you hospitalized until you can force yourself to stay out in the common area with the other patients for a significant portion of the day for several days.

- Hospital staff may check on you or interview you periodically.

- After you begin to recover and heal, you may be able to request to transition from the hospital to an outpatient facility. This is a separate facility that lets you receive treatment during the day, sometimes in the morning or the afternoon, which allows you to be primarily at home and sleep in your own bed.

Advice from Fellow Bipolar Warriors

Four bipolar individuals who have been in a psychiatric hospital talk about their experiences and offer advice.

Gary:

I was out of control, belligerent, and having hallucinations about being on a mission from God. I got in a fight in a bar with a bouncer who was giving me shit, and the cops came. I told them the bouncer was the devil. The police took me to a psychiatric hospital where I was involuntarily committed against my will. It took four days to heal up, but once I was back on my meds and had regained my balance, I told the doctor I had to get back to work and he signed my discharge papers. The nurses and staff were very good to me, smiling and telling me to take it easy and things would improve. I'm not sure what would have happened if I had not ended up in the hospital.

Ruth:

It is a really useful to have a friend who understands you are bipolar and will help you out if you get into trouble. During an extremely bad episode, I was involuntarily committed into a psychiatric hospital. After several days of taking medication and "coming to my senses," I called my friend Joe and told him where I was and that I needed to get out of there and back to work. Joe drove to the hospital, talked to my doctor, and vouched for me. He told the doctor I was a sales manager and had a good job. The doctor discharged me and I will be eternally grateful to Joe because he had my back and helped me out in my time of need.

Jane:

There's very little reason to go to a psychiatric hospital other than being suicidal or psychotic and wanting not to end up dead or injured. You do not receive therapy that's better than what you can get outside, and you'll almost certainly be heavily medicated. In fact, in many places you do not get individual therapy at all. If you want help, find a good therapist. It's a very incorrect idea that institutionalization is more intensive and will help you more. In fact, it will probably help you less. Being in your own home, in your own environment that you can control, facing the real problems of everyday life, you will be much more comfortable than staying in a place where you have no privacy, where nurses and staff treat you in a very condescending manner.

Scott:

The benefits of being in the hospital for me include: You are in a controlled environment in the event of physical violence or attempted suicide. It gives you a chance to regroup and get stabilized. It removes you from stress of relationships—spouse, significant other, or kids. It is a forgivable excuse for missing work and may keep you from getting fired. The staff and doctors generally treat you well and take your craziness in stride. The food is usually decent. Finally, it's amazing how fast you can regain balance by taking medication.

Don't Leave the Hospital Too Soon

If you find yourself in a psychiatric hospital, give yourself time to begin the recovery process and get back on your feet again. Depending on how bad of shape you are in, it may be worthwhile to stay in the hospital a couple of days longer to regain balance, rather than trying to get out as soon as possible. Once you get back out in the real world there is a long road ahead to full recovery. When you get home from the hospital, some of the same things that were stressing you out and were instrumental in triggering your episode may still be present. These stressors could be a spouse, roommate, your children, bills, a sick relative or other factors.

Additional Recovery Tips

- Do what the doctor and nurses tell you to do.

- Take the medications.

- Eat the food they provide.

- Sleep when you can.

- Make friends with another patient.

- Attend group therapy.

- If possible, go outside and get fresh air and sunshine.

- When it is offered, take a shower.

- Brush your teeth.

- Spend time in the common area instead of staying in your room most of the time—the nursing staff will be monitoring you, and staying isolated will extend your hospital stay.

- There are usually 2 or 3 patients who are in bad shape and acting out. Try to avoid them.

"*Perilous highs and desperate lows and extravagant flurries of mood are not always symptoms of a broken mind, but signs of a beating heart.*"

—Terri Cheney, Lawyer, Writer
Diagnosed with Bipolar Disorder

CHAPTER **12**

Legal Rights

The information presented in this chapter is an overview of legal rights for the mentally ill based on material found on the Internet. Legal rights for the mentally ill vary by state and by country. Always consult a lawyer who is versed in the laws where you live for legal advice.

Reference the following websites for detailed information about legal rights for the mentally ill:

https://mentalhealthrights.org/baker-act/

https://www.mhanational.org/issues/mental-health-rights

Legal Rights as an Employee

One of the serious repercussions of having bipolar disorder is that you may miss work, sometimes days or even weeks at a time, especially if hospitalization occurs. It is important to know that if you have bipolar disorder you often have disability rights with your employer and you can take measures to protect your job. This includes many essential benefits, including health insurance. If you find yourself in this situation, talk to Human Resources at your work (discreetly if possible) about your disability rights.

If the worst case happens and you become unemployed, you may still have rights with your employer. Consult a lawyer who specializes in employment law to find out if you have any recourse.

The Americans with Disabilities Act

The Americans with Disabilities Act (ADA) is a law that gives civil rights protection to individuals with disabilities. The ADA's legal definition of a disability is especially beneficial to those with bipolar disorder. According to the US Equal Employment Opportunity Commission, the ADA defines the term disability as "a physical or mental impairment that substantially limits a major life activity." Since bipolar disorder seriously affects people's ability to work, the ADA is of vital importance to those with the disorder. It ensures that people with bipolar disorder have rights at work and, in serious cases, provides them with disability benefits if they are unable to work due to their condition. Note that there are some restrictions that may apply in specific circumstances.

I was employed by different employers during two of my bipolar episodes, both of which involved me being hospitalized in a psychiatric hospital. I was fortunate in both cases. Once I came to my senses, I called my boss from the hospital and told him where I was and that I would get back to work as soon as I could. In each case my supervisor got Human Resources involved and I was thankfully able to keep my job.

To find out more about the ADA, consult the following website:

https://www.ada.gov/

The Laws Governing Involuntary Commitment

The information in this section is taken from the US National Library of Medicine National Institutes of Health (Testa, 2010). Keep in mind that each state and country has its own laws. Consult with a lawyer to ensure your legal rights are protected.

Involuntary commitment is a legal process through which an individual with symptoms of severe mental illness is court-ordered into a psychiatric hospital against their will. In general, laws restrict involuntary commitment to those who are "mentally ill" and/or under the influence of drugs or alcohol and are deemed to be in imminent danger of harming themselves or others.

If the police are called to a location, for whatever reason, and observe that you are suicidal, belligerent, threatening, or physically violent, they may take you to a psychiatric hospital or they may take you to jail. The immediate safety of you and anyone else is the primary concern. If you are bipolar, you should be taken to a psychiatric hospital for evaluation instead of a jail cell. However, many times the police won't realize you are bipolar. If you end up in jail due to a bipolar episode, tell the police and your lawyer that you are bipolar. You do have rights!

Reasons you can be involuntarily committed to a psychiatric hospital include:

1. You attempt suicide or attempt to harm yourself.

2. Many of us who are bipolar have a history of explosive behavior. Some may call this rage, mania, violence, or anger. If you become aggressive or violent

with others you can be involuntarily committed to a
psychiatric hospital.

3. A family member or someone else has you committed.

With most adverse bipolar behavior, those most affected are
usually the people who are closest to the bipolar individual, such
as family or friends. If you are having a bipolar episode and are
violent, suicidal, or making threats, a family member or someone else may decide to take action and have you committed to a
psychiatric hospital.

At the time, it will most likely seem harsh. These types of cases
of involuntary committal are usually accompanied by strong
emotions of the person committed and the person responsible for
the committing. It is highly possible that this person is taking
this action because they want to keep you, and themselves or
others, safe until the episode runs its course.

If someone is attempting to have you committed to a psychiatric
hospital against your will, get a lawyer. Bipolar episodes are
scary, confusing, and heart wrenching. It is to your advantage to
consult with someone who is not emotionally involved to steer
you through the legal issues and protect your legal rights.

In the rare case that the person who is attempting to have you involuntarily committed is trying to do you harm rather than help
you, keep your wits about you as much as possible and, again,
get a lawyer. Maybe you have not been getting along with that
person and he or she is on the warpath against you. Do your best
to remain calm and collected when you come before the judge
and convince them that there is no reason for you to be hospitalized. Explain that the person is making false accusations. Your
psychiatrist can be your best advocate in court.

Someone who decides to have you involuntarily committed to a psychiatric hospital must take the following steps:

1. They will file an affidavit with the clerk of superior court or magistrate of district court. The clerk or magistrate may issue an order to a law enforcement officer to take you into custody for examination by a qualified professional.

2. If the qualified professional finds that you are "mentally ill," you will most likely be taken to a psychiatric hospital.

3. When you arrive at the hospital you will be examined by a psychiatrist; if the hospital psychiatrist agrees with the first examiner that hospitalization is necessary, you will be admitted for observation and treatment. If they do not believe you should be in the hospital, you will be released.

4. A court hearing must be held no later than ten days after you are taken into custody. The hearing may be held either in the county where the commitment was initiated or at the hospital. Within a few days after you are admitted, a lawyer from the Office of Special Counsel will contact you. They will be your lawyer at the initial hearing. You may also hire a lawyer at your own expense. At the hearing, the judge will decide whether you should be treated in the hospital or discharged. If you are committed, the judge will decide how many days you will be kept in the hospital before another hearing must be held.

At the hearing, you have the following rights:

- The right to an attorney (you may hire your own, or an attorney can be provided for you).

- The right to be present at the hearing.

- The right to speak for yourself.

- The right to challenge what is said about you.

Legal Rights as a Patient in a Psychiatric Hospital

If you find yourself in a psychiatric hospital you have the following legal rights:

- It is your legal right that the hospital staff verbally explains and provides you with a written copy of the privacy policy, which gives you the right to choose whether you want to have visitors or not. If there are certain people you do not wish to see or hear from, the staff will ask you to write down their names, and they will make a note of it. If you do not wish to have outside friends, family members, employers, or anyone else know you're there, the staff will not make your presence known. They cannot legally verify in any way that you are a patient.

- You may immediately make telephone calls in order to get help with legal, medical, and mental health issues.

- You have the right to be visited by your clergy, lawyer, or physician at any time.

- You have the right to ask for help from hospital staff to make sure your rights are honored.

- You have the right to a civil commitment hearing, where a judge will decide whether you should be hospitalized by court order. You have the right to a court-appointed attorney at the court hearing. It is highly recommended to have a lawyer represent you at a court hearing to protect your legal rights.

- You have the right to an independent expert evaluation of your mental condition. If you can't afford this evaluation, it must be provided to you at no charge.

- You have the right to file a grievance with the hospital if you feel your rights have been violated. You can request the hospital's clients' rights officer to help you with filing your grievance.

- There is no time limit on a voluntary inpatient stay, and you may stay as long as you are willing and the medical staff believes there is a continued need for inpatient treatment. Again, a psychiatrist must discharge you.

- You may communicate by sealed mail with any individual, group, or agency.

- You have the right to be furnished with writing materials and reasonable postage.

- You have the right to receive mail, unless the head of the hospital determines it is medically harmful for you to receive mail.

- You have the right to receive visitors at regular hours, unless the head of the hospital determines it is medically harmful for you to receive visitors. The people who want to visit you must be notified immediately when you have recovered sufficiently to receive visitors.

- You have the right to wear your own clothes.

- You have the right to keep and use personal possessions (excluding anything deemed potentially harmful), including toilet articles.

- You have the right to request to be released from the hospital (Citizens Commission On Human Rights, 2020).

Legal Rights Regarding Medication Refusal

The standard procedure for dealing with medication refusal is to take the patient to court to legally force him or her to agree to take it. At the trial, the psychiatrist will explain exactly why they think you need to be hospitalized and why it is important for you to take medication. The judge then rules that you either have to take medication or don't have to take it. If so, this means that even if you refuse medication, you are legally obligated to take it. When you return to the psychiatric hospital, the doctors will offer you oral meds first, but if you will not take them, staff members will physically restrain you and administer the medication (Mind for better mental health, 2020).

How to Get Discharged From a Psychiatric Hospital

There is a process that must be followed for getting discharged from a psychiatric hospital. If you decide you want to be discharged, you cannot simply sign yourself out and leave when you decide to do so. You can request to be discharged by filling out the correct paperwork. If the request for discharge is approved, you will be allowed to leave within three workdays (Monday through Friday, not weekends or holidays). If you request to be discharged, there are three possible outcomes:

- The psychiatrist who is handling your case will agree that you can leave. When your request to be discharged is granted, you can leave at the end of seventy-two hours.

- There are cases in which someone who admitted themselves voluntarily to the psychiatric hospital is not allowed to leave of their own accord because the doctors and staff feel they are harmful to themselves or others. In this case, the hospital staff can ask the court to commit you. The hospital staff must file papers (an affidavit) within three workdays of receiving your "request of discharge" form. Your request for release becomes a request for a hearing. You will receive notice of a court hearing before a judge to determine whether a court order will be issued to keep you in the hospital. At the hearing, if the judge rules that you need to stay in the hospital you become an involuntary patient; otherwise you will be discharged.

- If the hospital does not file an affidavit within three workdays, you must be released immediately.

The Benefits of Having a Psychiatric Advance Directive

In order to protect yourself when you are experiencing a bipolar episode it is to your benefit to prepare a Psychiatric Advance Directive (PAD).

The PAD is a legal contract that allows you to choose and control in advance the care you will receive when you are mentally incapacitated and are unable to direct your own care during potential times of crisis. It serves to inform others about what treatment you do want or don't desire from psychiatrists or other mental health professionals in the event of a bipolar episode.

A PAD allows you to identify a person to whom you have given authority to make decisions on your behalf. Instead of having some stranger make the decisions, or have your family guess at what you would want, you can list your preferences.

Typical provisions in a PAD include the following:

- A list of symptoms you might experience during a bipolar episode.

- If you have children, the person or people you want to take care of them.

- Medication instructions, including a list of medications to be given ("I agree to these medications," or "I don't agree to these medications").

- Other information about medications, allergies, and side effects.

- Your choice of hospital.

- A list of emergency contacts (doctors, family member, or friend).

- Crisis precipitants: "The following may cause me to have a bipolar episode".

- Protective factors: "The following may help me avoid a mental health crisis".

- Preferences for ways the staff can help you while you are in the hospital.

- A list of people who can visit you in the hospital.

- What you want to be taken care of at your home if you are hospitalized: pets, plants, etc.

- Preferences as to whether you agree to special therapies —for example, electroconvulsive therapy.

Take a look at this website to see detailed information concerning a PAD:

https://www.nami.org/Advocacy/Policy-Priorities/Improve-Care/Psychiatric-Advance-Directives-(PAD)

Almost all states permit some form of legal Advance Directive. The following website allows you to download an Advance Directive for the state in which you live:

https://www.nhpco.org/patients-and-caregivers/advance-care-planning/advance-directives/downloading-your-states-advance-directive

"Make a bipolar battle plan, be a warrior, and fight the war against bipolar disorder. Victory means living a productive, happy life—and making your dreams come true!"
—Troy Steven, Writer, Aerospace Engineer
Diagnosed with Bipolar Disorder

Chapter 13

Winning The Bipolar War

C ontrolling the symptoms of bipolar disorder is an ongoing process. You must be relentless about getting necessary treatment and sticking to it. This book has instructed you how to create a bipolar battle plan that can help you learn to cope with your emotions, control negative thinking, minimize physical symptoms, deal with medication issues, manage problems within everyday life, and effectively treat your illness.

Remember that in war all battle plans can be altered. Be prepared to make changes to your plan when you find it necessary to do so. Change your plan as many times as needed until you achieve optimal mental and physical health.

Make the commitment to become a warrior, master the weapons in your bipolar battle plan, and win the war against bipolar disorder. Winning the war means never having another out-of-control bipolar episode that causes you to attempt suicide, harm yourself or others, end up in the psychiatric hospital, wreck your finances, lose your job, destroy relationships with friends and loved ones, or destroy your health. Winning the war means living a productive, happy life and making your dreams come true!

Bipolar Battle Plan Summary

- Bipolar Heal Thyself—take responsibility for your own treatment.

- Adopt the mindset of a warrior every day when you wake up.

- Create your personal bipolar battle plan. Make refinements as needed.

- Take action every day to further your plan.

- Monitor your mood (emotions and feelings).

- Be vigilant for bipolar symptoms.

- Make use of your support team.

- Launch your contingency plan sooner rather than later if you begin having a bipolar episode.

- Optimize your medications.

- Keep an eye out for side effects.

- Find a good psychiatrist whom you trust to treat your illness.

- Never stop learning about bipolar disorder.

- Strengthen and train your mind.

- Monitor your thoughts, and if they are negative change them to something more productive.

- Strengthen and train your body.

- Eat healthy and exercise. Drink lots of water.

- Do not abuse alcohol or drugs.

- Be cognizant of your legal rights.

- Don't ever settle for a mediocre life.

- Most importantly, never quit.

- Do whatever it takes to make your dreams come true!

YOU HAVE ALL THE WEAPONS YOU NEED— NOW FIGHT!

If you enjoyed this book and find it useful, please take a few moments to write a review on your favorite store, and please refer it to anyone you know that may benefit from the information inside.

You could be saving their life!

www.breakingbipolar.life

Your Personal Contingency Plan

Name: _____

Phone: _____

Address: _____

Support Team:	Name	Phone Number
Support Person 1		
Support Person 2		
Support Person 3		
Support Person 4		

24-Hour Emergency Numbers:
1) Immediate Emergency   Call 911
2) National Suicide Prevention Lifeline   1-800-273-8255
3) Mental Health Hotline   1-844-549-4266
4) Substance Abuse and Mental Health Helpline 1-800-662-4357
5) Crisis Text Line   Text 'HOME' to 741741

Current Medications:
1)
2)
3)

Medication Contingency Plan:
1)
2)
3)

Things That May Trigger a Relapse:
1)
2)
3)

Mania Early Warning Signs:
1)
2)
3)
Depression Early Warning Signs:
1)
2)
3)
If I develop any of these signs, I will:
1)
2)
3)
If my support people observe these signs, they may:
1)
2)
3)
These people can visit me in the hospital:
1)
2)
3)
I have a Psychiatric Advance Directive:
YES____ NO____

If "YES" attach it or note where it can be located. If "NO" one should be created in case of emergency.

Signature: _____
Date: _____

Remember to make a few copies of your Contingency Plan and give them to the people in your support team.

A PLAN IS USELESS IF NOT PUT INTO ACTION!

Resources

Americans with Disabilities Act (ADA) - a law that gives civil rights protection to individuals with disabilities.
https://www.ada.gov/

Area of brain linked to bipolar disorder pinpointed. Article in Science Daily discussing which areas of the brain are affected by bipolar disorder and their specific impact:
https://www.sciencedaily.com/releases/2017/01/170124144000.htm

Black Dog Institute: An educational, research, and clinical facility offering specialized expertise in mood disorders:
www.blackdoginstitute.org.au

BP Magazine: An excellent quarterly magazine about bipolar disorder that also comes in an online version and has a great online forum, making it easy to ask questions and get answers:
http://www.bphope.com

Depression and Bipolar Support Alliance
https://www.dbsalliance.org/support/

GoodRx. Prescription Discount Site:
www.goodrx.com

MHA. Mental Health America.
https://www.mhanational.org/issues/mental-health-rights

MHR. Mental Health Rights:

https://mentalhealthrights.org/baker-act/

National Institute of Mental Health (NIMH): The mission of the NIMH is to transform the understanding and treatment of mental illness through basic and clinical research, paving the way for prevention, recovery, and cure: http://www.nimh.nih.gov/index.shtml

NeuroStar TMS: Transcranial magnetic stimulation therapy is an FDA-cleared non-invasive medical treatment that is specifically for patients with major depression who have not benefited from initial antidepressant medication: http://neurostar.com/nondrug-treatment-for-depression/?gclid=CNa_na6hi7QCFQf0nAodBigAoA

http://www.youtube.com/NeurostarTMSTherapy

Newharbinger Publications: Excellent source on Mood Disorders: http://www.newharbinger.com

Non-Medical Treatment for Bipolar Disorder: http://www.ehow.com/facts_5685287_non_medical-treatment-bipolar-disorder.html#ixzz1xPMeZGdE

Psychiatric Advanced Directive (PAD) Explanation: https://www.nami.org/Advocacy/Policy-Priorities/Improve-Care/Psychiatric-Advance-Directives-(PAD)

Psychiatric Advance Director – Download Your State's Advance Directive Form: https://www.nhpco.org/patients-and-caregivers/advance-care-planning/advance-directives/downloading-your-states-advance-directive

The Best Bipolar Disorder Apps for 2019 can be found at the following website:

https://www.healthline.com/health/bipolar-disorder/top-iphone-android-apps#imoodjournal

The 7 Best Online Bipolar Disorder Support Groups of 2020:
https://www.verywellmind.com/best-online-bipolar-disorder-support-groups-4802211

Wikipedia is a free online encyclopedia with an excellent overview and description of bipolar disorder:
http://en.wikipedia.org/wiki/Bipolar_disorder

Bibliography

Alloy, Lauren. 2017. "Circadian Rhythm Dysregulation in Bipolar Spectrum Disorders." Accessed June 4, 2019. https://www.ncbi.nlm.nih.gov/pmc/articles/PMC6661150/

American Thyroid Association. 2020. "Prevalence and Impact of Thyroid Disease." Accessed January 15, 2020. https://www.thyroid.org/media-main/press-room/#:~:text=An%20estimated

Bailey, Eileen. 2019. "9 Famous People With Bipolar." Accessed May 15, 2020. https://www.healthcentral.com/slideshow/6-famous-people-bipolar-disorder

Bhandari, Smitha. 2019. "Celebrities With Bipolar Disorder." Accessed May 1, 2020. https://www.webmd.com/bipolar-disorder/ss/slideshow-celebrities-bipolar-disorder

Bhatia, Juhie. 2018. "13 Famous People With Bipolar Disorder." Accessed May 15, 2020. https://www.everydayhealth.com/bipolar-disorder-pictures/famous-people-with-bipolar-disorder.aspx

Bledsoe, Andrea. 2010. "Bipolar Disorder and Migraines." Accessed December 6, 2019. https://www.everydayhealth.com/hs/bipolar-depression/bipolar-disorder-and-migraines/

Bocchetta, Alberto. 2016. "Bipolar disorder and anti-thyroid antibodies: review and case series". Accessed June 5, 2019.
https://journalbipolardisorders.springeropen.com/articles/10.1186/s40345-016-0046-4

Bowden, Charles. 2005. "Bipolar Disorder and Work Loss." Accessed January 2, 2019.
https://journalbipolardisorders.springeropen.com/articles/10.1186/s40345-016-0046-4

Bressert, Steve. 2020. "Causes of Bipolar Disorder." Accessed March 5, 2020.
https://psychcentral.com/bipolar/bipolar-disorder-causes/

Burgess, Lana. 2016. "What is psychomotor agitation?" Accessed April 2, 2020.
https://www.medicalnewstoday.com/articles/319711

Burgess, Lana. 2019. "Is there a cure for Bipolar Disorder?" Accessed September 25, 2019.
https://www.medicalnewstoday.com/articles/324349.php

Carlos Castaneda's Don Juan Teachings. Accessed June 6, 2013.
http://www.prismagems.com/castaneda/donjuan8.html

Castaneda, Carlos. 1998. The Wheel of Time. New York: Pocketbooks.

Cerullo, Michael. 2007. "The prevalence and significance of substance use disorders in bipolar I and II disorder." Accessed January 6, 2020.
https://www.ncbi.nlm.nih.gov/pmc/articles/PMC2094705/

Chakrabarti, Subho. 2011. "Thyroid Functions and Bipolar Affective Disorder." Accessed December 1, 2019.
https://www.ncbi.nlm.nih.gov/pmc/articles/PMC3144691/

Chugani, Harry. 1987. "Positron emission tomography study of human brain functional development." Accessed December 5, 2019.
https://onlinelibrary.wiley.com/doi/abs/10.1002/ana.410220408

Cirino, Erica. 2019. "Can You Bipolar Disorder and an Anxiety Disorder at the Same Time?" Accessed February 8, 2020.
https://www.healthline.com/health/bipolar-and-anxiety

Citizens Commission On Human Rights. 2020. "Mental Health Declaration of Human Rights." Accessed March 5, 2020.
https://www.cchr.org/about-us/mental-health-declaration-of-human-rights.html

Clark, Luke. 2008. "Cognitive neuroscience and brain imaging in bipolar disorder." Accessed June 6, 2019.
https://www.ncbi.nlm.nih.gov/pmc/articles/PMC3181872/

Connell, Kelly. 2019. "Bipolar Disorder and Sexual Health." Accessed February 10, 2020.
https://www.healthline.com/health/bipolar-disorder/guide-sexual-health

Cooney, Lewis. 2017. "Overview of systematic reviews of therapeutic ranges: methodologies and recommendations for practice." Accessed June 6, 1019.
https://bmcmedresmethodol.biomedcentral.com/articles/10.1186/s12874-017-0363-z

Cronkleton, Emily. 2019. "Why Is Vitamin B Complex Important, and Where Do I Get It?" Accessed June 6, 2019.
https://www.healthline.com/health/food-nutrition/vitamin-b-complex

Dome, Peter. 2019. "Suicide Risk in Bipolar Disorder: A Brief Review." Accessed January 6, 2020.
https://www.ncbi.nlm.nih.gov/pmc/articles/PMC6723289/

Dutta, Sanchari. 2019. "What is Norepinephrine?" Accessed January 3, 2020.
https://www.news-medical.net/health/What-is-Norepinephrine.aspx

Feather, Ken. 1995. On The Toltec Path. VT: Bear & Company.

Foundations Recovery Network. 2020. "Untreated Bipolar Disorder Can Lead to Increased Risk of Domestic Violence." Accessed January 3, 2020.
https://dualdiagnosis.org/bipolar-disorder-and-addiction/domestic-violence-and-bipolar-disorder/#:~:text=a%20Manic%20Episode-
,Bipolar%20Disorder%20and%20Domestic%20Violence,to%20the%20bipolar%20person's%20partner

Ghaemi, Nassir. 2011. "Positive Aspects of Mental Illness: A Review on Bipolar Disorder." Accessed March 5, 2013.
http://www.bphope.com/item.aspx/915/accentuate-the-positive

Gibbons-Gwyn, Malinda. 2009. "Bipolar Disorder and Decision Making." Accessed February 9, 2020.
https://www.everydayhealth.com/bipolar-disorder/bipolar-disorder-and-decision-making.aspx#:~:text=Bipolar%20Disorder-
,Bipolar%20Disorder%20and%20Decision%20Making,responsibility%20and%20manage%20your%20emotions.&text=The%20dramatic%20mood%20swings%20of,particularly%20during%20a%20manic%20episode.

Hage, Mirella. 2011. "Thyroid Disorders and Diabetes Mellitus." Accessed June 5, 2019.
https://www.ncbi.nlm.nih.gov/pmc/articles/PMC3139205/#:~:text=Studies%20have%20found%20that%20diabetes,management%20of%20diabetes%20in%20patients

Harvey, Allison. 2015. "Interventions for Sleep Disturbance in Bipolar Disorder." Accessed December 2, 2019. https://www.ncbi.nlm.nih.gov/pmc/articles/PMC4347516/

Haycock, Dean. 2010. "The Everything Health Guide to Adult Bipolar Disorder." MA: Adams Media.

Healthessentials. 2020. "Why Having a Pet Can Boost Your Mood and Keep Your Brain Healthy." Accessed May 1, 2020. https://health.clevelandclinic.org/why-having-a-pet-of-any-kind-may-boost-your-mood-and-keep-your-brain-healthy/

HelpGuide. 2020. "Bipolar Disorder Signs and Symptoms." Accessed January 29, 2020. https://www.helpguide.org/articles/bipolar-disorder/bipolar-disorder-signs-and-symptoms.htm

HelpGuide. 2020. "Bipolar Disorder Treatment." Accessed February 7, 2020. https://www.helpguide.org/articles/bipolar-disorder/bipolar-disorder-treatment.htm

Hibar, D. 2017. "Bipolar disorder affects brain regions controlling inhibition, emotion." Accessed June 6, 2019. https://www.healio.com/news/psychiatry/20170605/bipolar-disorder-affects-brain-regions-controlling-inhibition-emotion

Hill, Napoleon. 1997. Napoleon Hill's Keys to Success. New York: Plume.

Hill, Napoleon 2012. Think and Grow Rich. Aristeus-Books.

Hook, Debra-Lynn. 2015. "How Seasonal Pattern Affects Bipolar Disorder." Accessed May 1, 2020. https://www.everydayhealth.com/depression/seasonal-depression-and-bipolar.aspx

Hornbacher, Marya. 2008. Madness: A Bipolar Life. New York: First Mariner Books.

Huizen, Jennifer. 2019. "Medications for bipolar disorder: What you should know." Accessed January 3. 2020. https://www.medicalnewstoday.com/articles/324388

Jamison, Kay. 1996. An Unquiet Mind. New York: First Vintage Books.

Jamison, Kay. 1994. Touched with Fire. New York: Free Press Paperbacks.

Kessler, R. C. 2005. "The Numbers Count: Mental Disorders in America." Accessed March 10, 2013. https://www.nimh.nih.gov/health/statistics/index.shtml

Kildare, Sasha. 2020. "The Essential Guide To Maintaining Friendships With Bipolar." Accessed March 6, 2020. https://www.bphope.com/friendships-bipolar-maintaining/

King, Stephen. 2018. The Outsider. New York: Simon & Shuster, Inc.

Krans, Brian. 2017. "Diagnosis Guide for Bipolar Disorder." Accessed September 25, 2019. https://www.healthline.com/health/bipolar-disorder/bipolar-diagnosis-guide

Kvarnstorm, Elisabet. 2018. "Understanding Bipolar Disorder Triggers and How to Prevent Them." Accessed December 2, 2019. https://www.bridgestorecovery.com/blog/understanding-bipolar-disorder-triggers-and-how-to-prevent-them/

Leech, Joe. 2018. "11 Proven Health Benefits of Garlic". Accessed June 3, 2019.

https://www.healthline.com/nutrition/11-proven-health-benefits-of-garlic#section1

Leech, Joe. 2018. "10 Evidence-Based Health Benefits of Cinnamon." Accessed June 3, 2019.
https://www.healthline.com/nutrition/10-proven-benefits-of-cinnamon#section10

Legg, Timothy. 2019. "Energy level Combatting Bipolar Disorder Related Fatigue." Accessed February 5, 2020.
https://www.healthline.com/health/bipolar-disorder/guide-fatigue#sleep-smarter

Legg, Timothy. 2020. "What Causes Bipolar Disorder?" Accessed May 9, 2020.
https://www.healthline.com/health/bipolar-disorder/bipolar-causes

Legg, Timothy. 2019. "What Does It Mean to Have a Parent with Bipolar Disorder?" Accessed January 3, 2019.
https://www.healthline.com/health/bipolar-disorder/how-to-deal-with-a-bipolar-parent

Leonard, Jayne. 2019. "Bipolar Type Definitions." Accessed January 15, 2020.
https://www.medicalnewstoday.com/articles/324437#types-of-bipolar-disorder

Link, Rachael. 2020. "8 Surprising Health Benefits of Cloves." Accessed April 9, 2020.
https://www.healthline.com/nutrition/benefits-of-cloves

MacGill, Markus. 2019. "How does bipolar disorder affect memory?" Accessed February 4, 2020.
https://www.medicalnewstoday.com/articles/314328

Madhusoodanan, Jyoti. 2019. "Complications of Hypothyroidism." Accessed November 1, 2019.
https://www.healthline.com/health/hypothyroidism/complications#1

Mann, Andrea. 2016. "From fighting colon cancer to arthritis, 8 great benefits of curry." Accessed June 3, 2019.
http://home.bt.com/lifestyle/wellbeing/like-a-bit-of-spice-8-great-health-benefits-of-curry-11363994131863

Mariant, David. "Surviving Bipolar". Accessed February 14, 2013.
http://www.survivingbipolar.com/green_suicide.htm#2

Martin, B. 2006. "Phases and Symptoms of Bipolar Disorder." Psych Central. Accessed January 14, 2012.
https://psychcentral.com/lib/phases-and-symptoms-of-bipolar-disorder/

Mayo Clinic, 2018. "Bipolar Disorder." Accessed January 2, 2019.
https://www.mayoclinic.org/diseases-conditions/bipolar-disorder/diagnosis-treatment/drc-20355961

Mayo Clinic. 2020. "Bipolar Disorder." Accessed February 7, 2020.
https://www.mayoclinic.org/diseases-conditions/bipolar-disorder/symptoms-causes/syc-20355955

Mayo Clinic. 2020. "Bipolar Disorder." Accessed February 5, 2020.
https://www.mayoclinic.org/diseases-conditions/bipolar-disorder/symptoms-causes/syc-20355955

Mayo Clinic. 2020. "Hyperthyroidism (overactive thyroid)." Accessed March 3, 2020.

https://www.mayoclinic.org/diseases-conditions/hyperthyroid-ism/symptoms-causes/syc-20373659

Mayo Clinic, 2017. "Vitamin D". Accessed March 9, 2020.
https://www.google.com/search?q=benefits+of+vita-min+d&rlz=1C1NCHA_enUS589US598&oq=benefits+of+vita-min+d&aqs=chrome..69i57j0l7.10678j0j7&sourceid=chrome&ie=UTF-8

McElroy, S. L. 2002. "Correlates of Overweight and Obesity in 644 Patients with Bipolar Disorder." Accessed September 2, 2012.
https://pubmed.ncbi.nlm.nih.gov/11926719/

McIntosh, James. 2018. "What is serotonin and what does it do?" Accessed January 3, 2020.
https://www.medicalnewstoday.com/articles/232248

McQuillan, Susan. 2019. "Is Bipolar Disorder Increasing Your Risk of Developing Heart Disease?" Accessed January 12, 2020.
https://www.psycom.net/bipolar-disorder-and-heart-disease/

MEDTV, 2020. "Wellbutrin Side Effects." Accessed November 12, 2012.
http://depression.emedtv.com/wellbutrin/wellbutrin-side-ef-fects.html

Mert, Derya. 2013. "Perspectives on reasons of medication non-adherence in psychiatric patients." Accessed September 25, 2019.
https://www.ncbi.nlm.nih.gov/pmc/articles/PMC4298301/

Mind for better mental health. 2020. "Psychiatric medication." Accessed April 10, 2020.
https://www.mind.org.uk/information-support/drugs-and-treat-ments/medication/your-right-to-refuse-medication/

Monson, Kristi. 2007. "Risperdal Side Effects." Accessed April 10, 2013.
http://schizophrenia.emedtv.com/risperdal/risperdal-side-effects.html

Najafi-Vosough, Roya. 2016. "Recurrence in Patients with Bipolar Disorder and Its Risk Factors." Accessed June 5, 2019.
https://www.ncbi.nlm.nih.gov/pmc/articles/PMC5139952/

Narita, Kosuke. 2011. "Volume Reduction of Ventromedial Prefrontal Cortex in Bipolar II Patients with Rapid Cycling: A Voxel-Based Morphometric Study." Accessed July 7, 2013.
https://www.sciencedirect.com/science/article/abs/pii/S0278584610004616

National Institute of Mental Health. 2019. "Bipolar Disorder Statistics." Accessed January 7, 2020.
https://www.nimh.nih.gov/health/statistics/index.shtml

Natural Endocrine Solutions. 2018. "Fluoride, Bromide, Chloride and Thyroid Health." Accessed January 3, 2020.
https://www.naturalendocrinesolutions.com/articles/fluoride-bromide-chloride-and-thyroid-health/

Nauert, Rick. 2018. "Link Between Bipolar and Hypertension." Accessed December 10, 2018.
https://psychcentral.com/news/2010/06/14/link-between-bipolar-and-hypertension/14542.html

Newton, Phil. 2009. "What is Dopamine?" Accessed January 3, 2020.
https://www.psychologytoday.com/us/blog/mouse-man/200904/what-is-dopamine

Propst, Stephen. 2019. "10 Ways to Repair Your Self Esteem." Accessed January 3, 2020.
https://www.bphope.com/strengthening-your-self-esteem/

Purse, Marcia. 2009. "Anxiety Medications: Bipolar Disorder Medications Library." Accessed January 16, 2013.
http://bipolar.about.com/od/sedatives/a/anxiety_medications.htm

Purse, Marcia. 2020. "What is a Manic Episode?" Accessed June 1, 2020.
https://www.verywellmind.com/how-to-recognize-a-manic-or-hypomanic-episode-380316

Robertson, Ruairi. 2018. "13 Benefits of Taking Fish Oil." Accessed April 3, 2019.
https://www.healthline.com/nutrition/13-benefits-of-fish-oil

Rodriguez, Diana. 2012. "Bipolar Disorder: Regain Your Self-Esteem." Accessed February 2, 2020.
https://www.everydayhealth.com/hs/bipolar-depression/self-esteem-with-bipolar-disorder/

Ruiz, Miguel. 1997. "The Four Agreements." San Rafael: Amber-Allen Publishing. Accessed May 8, 2020.
https://www.miguelruiz.com/the-four-agreements

Sachs, Gary. 2008. "Are Men or Women More Likely to Develop Bipolar Disorder?" Accessed June 6, 2013.
http://abcnews.go.com/Health/BipolarRiskFactors/story?id=4356077

Sauer, Patrick. 2016. "Manic Spending Puts Bipolar Patients at Risk for Financial Woes." Accessed December 19, 2019.
https://www.health.com/condition/bipolar/manic-spending-puts-bipolar-patients-at-risk-for-financial-woes

Sheehan, Jan. 2008. "Coping With Bipolar Mood Swings." Accessed January 3, 2019.
https://www.everydayhealth.com/bipolar-disorder/bipolar-disorder-mood-swings.aspx

Smith, Melinda. 2019. "Depression Symptoms and Warning Signs." Accessed April 4, 2020.
https://www.helpguide.org/articles/depression/depression-symptoms-and-warning-signs.htm

Streit, Lizzie. 2018. "10 Health Benefits of Cardamom, Backed by Science." Accessed June 3, 2019.
https://www.healthline.com/nutrition/cardamom-benefits

Surks, Martin. 2019. "Lithium and the thyroid." Accessed December 3, 2019.
https://www.uptodate.com/contents/lithium-and-the-thyroid

Swartz, Holly. 2014. "Psychotherapy for Bipolar Disorder in Adults: A Review of the Evidence." Accessed December 5, 2019.
https://www.ncbi.nlm.nih.gov/pmc/articles/PMC4536930/

Tartakovsky, Margarita. 2020. "Bipolar Disorder Fact Sheet." Accessed April 4, 2020.
https://psychcentral.com/bipolar/bipolar-disorder-fact-sheet/

Testa, Megan. 2010. "Civil Commitment in the United States." Accessed January 12, 2020.
https://www.ncbi.nlm.nih.gov/pmc/articles/PMC3392176/

The Bledsoe Firm. 2017. "Marriage (or Deciding to Divorce) When Your Spouse Suffers from Bipolar Disorder." Accessed January 2, 2019.
https://www.fieldsdennis.com/wp-content/uploads/2018/03/Marriage-or-Deciding-to-Divorce-When-Your-Spouse-Suffers-from-Bipolar-Disorder.pdf

Thompson, Dennis. 2010. "Can Bipolar Lead to Diabetes?" Accessed November 12, 2012.

http://www.everydayhealth.com/bipolar-disorder/can-bipolar-disorder-lead-to-diabetes.aspx

University of Michigan General Research Center. 2005. "Evidence of Brain Chemistry Abnormalities in Bipolar Disorder." Accessed March 4, 2013.
http://bipolar.about.com/cs/menu_science/a/press_umich0210.htm

University of Texas Health Science Center. 2017. "Area of brain linked to bipolar disorder pinpointed." Accessed June 6, 2019.
https://www.sciencedaily.com/releases/2017/01/170124144000.htm

Vann, Madeline. 2017. "9 Most Common Triggers for Bipolar Mood Episodes." Accessed January 3, 2020.
https://www.everydayhealth.com/bipolar-disorder-pictures/biggest-triggers-of-bipolar-mood-swings.aspx

Vann, Madeline. 2010. "Are People with Bipolar Disorder Dangerous?" Accessed March 5, 2013.
http://www.everydayhealth.com/bipolar-disorder/are-people-with-bipolar-disorder-dangerous.aspx

WebMD. 2019. "Everyday Tips for Living With Bipolar Disorder." Accessed March 3, 2020.
https://www.webmd.com/bipolar-disorder/guide/living-healthy-life-with-bipolar#1

WebMD. 2019. "Bipolar Disorder and Sleep Problems." Accessed January 7, 2020.
https://www.webmd.com/bipolar-disorder/guide/bipolar-disorder-and-sleep-problems#1

WebMD. 2019. "Bipolar Disorder." Accessed March 3, 2020.
https://www.webmd.com/bipolar-disorder/mental-health-bipolar-disorder#1

WebMD. 2019. "Causes of Bipolar Disorder." Accessed March 5, 2020.
https://www.webmd.com/bipolar-disorder/guide/bipolar-disorder-causes#1

WebMD. 2019. "Depression in Bipolar Disorder: What You Can Do." Accessed March 10, 2020.
https://www.webmd.com/bipolar-disorder/guide/depression-symptoms#1

WebMD, 2020. "Bipolar Episodes With Mixed Features." Accessed March 3, 2020.
https://www.webmd.com/bipolar-disorder/guide/mixed-bipolar-disorder#1

WebMD, 2020. "Psychotherapy for Bipolar Disorder." Accessed March 6, 2020.
https://www.webmd.com/bipolar-disorder/guide/psychotherapy-bipolar-disorder#1

WebMD. 2010. "The benefits of Vitamin C." Accessed March 2, 2020.
https://www.webmd.com/diet/features/the-benefits-of-vitamin-c#1

WebMD. 2020. "Bipolar Disorder and Self-Injury." Accessed January 3, 2020.
https://www.webmd.com/bipolar-disorder/guide/bipolar-disorder-self-injury#1

Woods, 2015. "Diabetes in Bipolar Disorder Takes Its Toll." Accessed January 7, 2020.
https://www.psychiatrictimes.com/view/diabetes-bipolar-disorder-takes-its-toll

Young, A.H. 2013. "Physical health of patients with bipolar disorder." Accessed September 25, 2019.
https://onlinelibrary.wiley.com/doi/pdf/10.1111/acps.12117

York, Susan. 2017. "Understanding Psychosis in Bipolar Disorder." Accessed January 3, 2020.
https://www.healthline.com/health/bipolar-disorder/bipolar-psychosis

Zelman, Kathleen. 2010. "The benefits of Vitamin C." Accessed March 2, 2020.
https://www.webmd.com/diet/features/the-benefits-of-vitamin-c#1

Index

periods of irritability or anger, 19
planning process, 15, 16
plans are sound, 17
point of no return, 22
pointers for finding a new
    psychiatrist, 90
polar mood swings, 19
polar opposites, 19, 46
Positron Emission Tomography, 63
prepare yourself for the battles
    ahead, 45
prevent additional episodes, 20, 59
pros of the medicine, 30
Psychiatric Advance Directive, 163,
    172
psychiatric hospital, 143
psychomotor agitation, 50
psychotic, 49, 52, 70, 151

R

racing speech and thoughts, 19
Recommendations, 22, 24, 26
Recovery does not happen overnight,
    130
Reducing self-importance frees up
    energy, 101
refine and make improvements, 17
replace it with a new plan, 17
Risperdal, 79
ritual casting off of bad habits, 120
ruminating over past events, 26
running your personal bipolar
    marathon, 111

S

Seasonal pattern, 53
self-medicating with drugs and
    alcohol, 27, 120
self-respect, 2
serious and life-threatening, 19
Seroquel, 3, 22, 24
Serotonin, 62
seven negative emotions, 102
seven positive emotions, 102

shifts in mood, 19, 46
shorter life span, 15
skills necessary for warfare, 30
sky-rocketing out of control, 21, 37
solid support system, 69
specific brand of bipolar disorder, 19,
    58
speeding up your recovery, 29
spend money recklessly, 15
stalk yourself, 107
statistics, 2, 23, 60
steps you can take to face fear, 110
stop trying to make yourself right and
    others wrong, 108
strong support system, 15, 140
subconscious mind, 102
Substance Abuse and Mental Health
    Helpline (1-800-662-4357), 22
successful treatment of bipolar
    disorder, 15, 140
suicide attempt, 2, 3
Sun Tzu, The Art Of War, 19
swallowing all of my medications, 22
sweet spot, 68
switch has been thrown, 22
symptoms vary widely, 19, 58

T

tailor your battle plan, 16
taking control of your bipolar
    disease, 59
Ted Turner, 8
The Good Stuff, 9
The Outsider by Stephen King, 120
the true nature of bipolar illness, 60
the worst hell I ever imagined, 4
Therapy can help you to, 137
there is no test to specifically detect
    bipolar disorder., 69
Things to know if you are in a
    psychiatric hospital, 147
Think and Grow Rich, 102
Three ways to check yourself into a
    psychiatric hospital, 144

Personal Notes

Made in the USA
Monee, IL
11 March 2021

62440037R00132